BEING BLISS

(2nd Edition)

by Indigo Ocean

Copyright © 2011 Indigo Ocean

All rights reserved.

ISBN-13: 978-0615460215 – Bodhi Press

ISBN-10: 0615460216

DEDICATION

This book is dedicated to you, for without your call the response could not have been sent through me.

CONTENTS

Introduction   7

The Three Keys to Bliss

1. Miracle Manifestation   19
2. Love in Action   41
3. Beyond Conditions   59

The Three Supporting Powers

4. The Power of Conviction   73
5. The Power of Self-knowledge   91
6. The Power of Innocence   107

Living as Bliss: Tools & Techniques

7. Habit   127
8. Mind   137
9. Body   159
10. Emotions   181
11. Spirit   197
12. Relationship   217

About the Author   243

INTRODUCTION

Every person wants to be free, but some want it more than others. The amount of freedom we experience in life will directly relate to the amount of courage we put into action. It must mean more to us to be free than to live behind an illusion of safety. Our vulnerability must not intimidate us so thoroughly that we imprison ourselves behind a fortress of self-defense, habitually anticipating every conceivable threat and dancing the dance of avoidance with every step. That is the path of suffering, and it is not the path I want you to walk.

These bodies we each call "me" are slowly dying. We are in fact moving towards death with every moment of our lives. We live as if we aren't most of the time. We try to overlook it, but our fear of death does not go away simply because we bury it deep within our unconscious. Instead it festers there, coming out in all sorts of unexpected ways, slowly draining away our life.

You cannot fully live while the focus of your life is clinging to what you have and avoiding loss. There is overwhelming stress involved in that. This stress is despair. It is sloth. It is anger. It is illness. It is suicide. It is violence. But if there is sufficient courage you will pursue and embrace the wisdom and skillful means you need to end your self-defensive stress and win the freedom to grow through joy.

For this courage to arise, two things are needed. You must encounter love so that you have some glimmer of faith in basic human goodness and you must want freedom badly enough. Living small and scared must hurt badly enough for you to make the effort and take the risks involved, including facing some truths about yourself, so that you can learn to manifest the fulfillment of your hopes and dreams and be a blessing to this world. The cost of freedom is full personal responsibility, and that is what many people fear most.

In this book I am going to show you that it is possible to live a life in full awareness of human vulnerability and responsibility and do so with joy. More than that, I am going to teach you how. It is from experience that I speak to you, so you can trust that what I say is practical and effective.

Fear and hopelessness ruled my life for decades, but they don't have a grip on me anymore. For years now I have embraced a different way of living that has blessed me with the most important kind of freedom there is, the freedom to grow on a path of joy instead of one of suffering.

I am a happy person. I am a truly, ecstatic, joyful person. And that is not because these years have been easy. In this time period I have suffered much pain and loss. During these years I have seen someone I loved slowly die. During these years, I have found myself in New York City to experience the destruction of the towers, witness the needless deaths of all those innocent people, and watch the militarization of the city for a year thereafter. During these years, more than once I have received news that has shocked me to my core and sent my mind spinning in search of alternative truths. Yet through it all I have remained a truly blissful person.

To be bliss doesn't mean to be untouched. It's not a state of detachment. On the contrary, you feel more. You don't hide from any of what you experience so you feel all of what has always been there. This means you find the horror of life along with the beauty. It means you are fully alive now while you have a chance to be.

I wrote this book because I am dying. At the time I began it I was convinced by my doctor that my death was imminent. That turned out to be untrue, but by then I was already half way through writing it so I decided to finish. This body really is dying anyway, though I will likely have another 50 years or so before I decide to "walk off the set."

This book is an offering to you on behalf of the All Pervading Light. Here I refer to it as "the All Pervading Light," but in other places I will say "God, Goddess, Ultimate All, Source, Infinite, Spirit, Unity, Luminous Emptiness" and a host of other labels. In seeking to name that which is beyond all concepts, what word or phrase can really capture the Truth? So here is an opening disclaimer. I cannot tell you the Truth.

If you read this book with full attention and an open mind and use the techniques found herein, you will experience the truth as it is able to reveal itself to you through me right now. In the process of conveying this to you, I will have to use words, but any words can only attempt to evoke the truth, not be it. Truth is lived. You are living it right now, but are you self aware? Let us take this journey together as partners in discovery.

I believe that everything in this book is something that is worth the time of anyone choosing to live fully while they can. Oh I know, you probably have a few good years left in you, maybe 50 or so – but then even you will have to walk off the set, so let's not waste any time. The time for you to go beyond confusion, despair, shame, fear, lack, and discontent is now. The time for enduring bliss has arrived.

All that I suggest you do, I've done myself and that's how I know that it's effective. I've also seen many clients use these techniques successfully, so I know it isn't just me. They work, and that is the test for me as to whether they should be shared. I can't offer truths. I don't know the truth. I can only offer an approach to living that will infuse your life experience with joy, peace, abundance, and love.

It doesn't matter where you are in life as you begin using these techniques. No matter how low you think you are, how truly justified your sadness, despair and grief may be, I promise you that being bliss is an absolute possibility for you. In fact, bliss is your true nature. I know because I once lived in the pits so long that it became my idea of "normal," yet I came out of it. I can tell you firsthand that there is no depth that is beyond recovery.

My Story

If you had asked me about the average person's chances for happiness 11 years ago I would have offered a tentative answer. My answer would have come from hope, not knowledge. I believed from the words of others that happiness was possible, but I had never known it personally.

Throughout my childhood I suffered from clinical depression. I attempted suicide the first time at only nine years of age. The last attempt was at the age of 21. What prevented further attempts after that was not so much that I had a reason to live as that because I was hospitalized on the last attempt my younger sister found out about my suicidal behavior. I was so concerned that she might learn from me to give up on life that I realized I could never kill myself so long as she lived.

What would become of her if her sister, who had for so many years spoken so passionately about her worth and possibility, was to give up on the worth and possibility of her own life? Like it or not, I had to stay in this body until chance provided me with a good enough exit to preserve her sense of hope.

In the meantime, I figured I'd best try some new approaches in pursuit of happiness. After many false paths, I finally came to volunteer at Glide Memorial Church in San Francisco. I was motivated by a recollection that when I was a teenage volunteer I had experienced some minor degrees of enjoyment within the course of service work. It was worth the time to explore that avenue again.

The first volunteer position I took at Glide was working with the children in the computer lab. I went a few weeks and it was wonderful to be with them, surrounded at last by innocence. I thought I was giving them enough love and that it was all going quite smoothly. Then one day a little Vietnamese boy asked me how I had liked the church service the day before. I told him that I hadn't been there. He asked why I missed it. I told him that I didn't go to church, but only wanted to volunteer to help him and the other children. He was clearly puzzled.

I realized then that the Sunday services meant so much to the children I was helping that I could not call myself committed to them without going to at least one service so that I knew what experience they were having there. So the next Sunday I got myself up much earlier than a Sunday morning generally meant to me and off to church I went.

To my surprise, I felt comfortable there. I went in jeans and as I looked around I saw many young people, many people in casual attire, and people of various races. Everyone was pretty friendly and welcoming and it was easy to see myself getting in and out without any unpleasant experiences, which was rare for me, each scene of my life having pretty much been fraught with pain up to that point.

Then a visiting artist stepped up to sing. Her name was Denise Austin. I recalled the name from childhood and knew I was in for a treat. I had picked the right Sunday to drop in for a look at Glide's service, for sure.

As she sang, the excitement of star power quickly gave way to the awe of hearing the voice of God speaking to me. She sang, "Come on home. It is time to come home to God." Such simple words, but they reached into the very core of me. It literally felt as if it was God singing directly to me, asking me to please come back to Him, to please make peace with Him.

By this time in my life, after 27 years of depressive agony in all social situations, I had nearly perfected the ability to hide my emotions from those around me, but all my discipline broke down in that moment. Tears rolled uncontrollably down my face as I felt something opening within me. As it opened, in rushed a current of light that seemed to cleanse the corners of my heart. I was enveloped in a field of warmth, tenderness and safety as if for the first time.

At home later that day, I remembered that I had once had a very close relationship with God. Up until the age of 9 I had spent hours talking to God each day. When the other children were out playing, I stayed in my room to be with God instead. Already suffering from undiagnosed depression, I felt overwhelmed by the world of free play. Only at school was there enough order supplied by the teacher for me to have enough safety to come out of my shell. And in that arena I was a star. But outside the confines of the class, I was thoroughly incompetent in understanding life or knowing how to respond in pretty much any situation. Afternoons with God and long, deep sleep cycles each night were how I survived until I was old enough to direct my own studies.

Once I discovered that I could lose myself in an endless series of library books, I was off God. I don't know why I made that choice, but somehow I seemed to have forgotten my personal relationship with him and come to think of him only in terms of the judgmental "jealous" god my parents were trying to teach me about. I didn't like that God. He didn't make me feel safe at all. The world of ideas felt much safer. Like many before me, I became a somber, withdrawn, bookworm at war with the very notion of God. By age 19 I had come home from my Ivy League college announcing myself as an agnostic.

Though the years before that had been very difficult, in retrospect I realize that was the beginning of the truly dark times. Only after I made peace with the personal God and began the process of healing did I realize the cost the war had extracted from me. I had made a God out of the intellect and looked to the intellectual as if following in the footsteps of Christ himself. And a cruel and vicious heaven it was indeed.

Once I made my peace and began again on the path of seeking the truth of life and the keys to happiness not through the intellect, but through the heart, I threw off my false gods. It was at that time that I began to study and practice wholeheartedly the very insights and techniques that fill the pages of this book.

I began life with a physical condition and family history that magnetized me towards depression. Some might say that only through medication could I ever be healthy or happy. But I stand here now as a truly happy person, happier than most and even able to bring the light of happiness into the lives of those around me. I don't take drugs, not Prozac, alcohol, marijuana, or even much caffeine, and I swear to you that what I have done you can do too.

The turning point for me came when I experienced the unconditional love of the All-Pervading Light moving through another person, the guest singer at Glide. I was then able to find the courage within myself to choose life over safety. As beaten down as I was, I chose to face the possibility of even more pain for the chance at something greater. I regained hope that maybe, just maybe, this was a kind and loving world that I could emotionally face without being destroyed. I then seized the opportunity and applied all my focus, skill and energy towards learning the secrets of the happy people, hoping that if anyone could be happy so could I.

It is out of my love for you that I write this book chronicling what I have learned, pointing out the principles behind the lessons, and guiding you in their application. May my voice reach you wherever you are and remind you that you too are loved. You are not so odd that you have been excluded from the flow of Divine Love. You simply need to learn how to be happy, and were never fully taught that.

Through the inspiration and insight of this book, may you find the courage to face what must be faced, learn what must be learned, and do what must be done to joyfully embrace your responsibilities as a Divine creator within a vulnerable physical vehicle. I want you to give it your all. I know you can do it.

What's Inside

Work at this book for a month. Give it 30 days of your wholehearted effort and be willing to let it change you. Study and contemplate the insights in the three chapters of the first section, the keys to happiness, and the following three chapters of the second section, the powers that activate those keys. Practice the techniques in the next 5 chapters making up the third section, skill development, so that you can access the full potential of the most essential key to happiness. And finally, rest within the container that is found within the final chapter on Relationship.

I write this book as both a professional and a fellow traveler on the road of self-healing. I am a dedicated spiritual practitioner and have studied Buddhism over the last 15 years, training under some of the most advanced teachers in the world. I have studied a number of other spiritual paths as well, in addition to holding a Master's degree in Integral Counseling Psychology. All of that experience influences my point of view.

I have also offered one-on-one assistance to others as an energy and guidance channel. A channel is someone who is able to connect with their higher self so strongly that they are able to receive energetic transmissions and clear information through the connection. Though a connection with the higher self is the pathway, the source of the information varies. Common sources include the higher self, angels/spirit guides – and some would even include life-forms from other planets on the list, though I have never knowingly had such contact.

You will find a couple channeled passages in the pages of this book, though I try not to lean heavily in that direction. I know some of you are skeptical about the entire field of channeling and I believe it is possible to convey most of the wisdom of my guides using my own words. Whenever I feel something would be lost in translation, however, you will find italicized "thought transmissions" I have channeled while writing this book.

A great deal of the insights that infuse this book are a synthesis of information I have channeled during individual sessions with clients. So often when I am sharing a guide's wisdom with someone my intellect will silently be running in the background, saying, "I need to remember that myself," or "I am going to do that spiritual practice sometimes too." This is the difference between being a spiritual teacher and a spiritual channel. Just because I can channel the information, doesn't mean I have learned the lesson. I am learning as teaching comes through me. (I love having work that allows me to be a full-time student of my favorite subject, spiritual growth, without taking out any more student loans.) I periodically re-read this book myself to keep myself focused on the most essential lessons for my own spiritual development.

If you are more comfortable with humans than with spirit guides, rest assured that despite the inclusion of wisdom from channeling sessions there is still quite a bit of everyday-people personality in this book. You will also find a little quantum physics interwoven with corresponding insights from spiritual traditions. (I did graduate from a science and math high school, after all.) And more than anything else, you will find stories from life.

I believe that the best teaching comes from example and as I have had to practice and learn the wisdom of the beings I channel in order to see countless blessings unfold in my life, I have many stories I have collected along the way. I'm happy to share those life lessons with you.

Immerse yourself in this journey. Give it a month. And I pray, by the end of the 30 days, if not before, may you be peaceful and at ease. May you be full of love and laughter. May you be happy.

Try This For 30 Days:

Create a journal to chronicle your journey of growth as you work with this material. You will be glad you did later, especially once you get used to living in your bliss. You will enjoy seeing how you progressed and how far you came. It may seem hard to believe now, but it is likely you will actually forget what it was like to be as you are now after just six short months of living life differently.

Any notebook will do, but please start with a blank one purchased just for this purpose. On page one write, "My intentions for what I will gain through reading this book and doing the exercises." Then write whatever you truly intend. On the last page write, "In Summary, this is what I have learned/gained." Obviously this last page will be filled in once you have completed the process.

Many blessings on your journey.

1 MIRACLE MANIFESTATION

Recently, when I faced the possibility of my imminent death, the clarity that came to me was that I wanted to live longer so that I could help more people. I was not ready to go because I felt so much had been put into me that had yet to come back out to bless the world. So much more was possible that my early death seemed a terrible waste and this made me very sad. I wanted life.

Part of me argued that I should surrender to God's will. If I was to live so that I could serve Him/Her/It by serving the world, so be it. If God had other plans for me then I was to trust that those must be greater plans and joyfully submit to them. I should die in peace without resistance.

Back and forth. Back and forth. Finally I have come to this. I care. I can say a prayer that God's will be my will. I can pray that I want whatever is wanted by Universal Wisdom. But what if the Universe has no opinion on the matter? What if it is random whether I live or die unless I choose?

So I was leaning in the direction of personal choice. The decision was finalized when I realized that if God wanted me dead, no matter how I exerted my influence, I was a goner. But if there was no greater plan it mattered a great deal whether I exercised the power of choice. I then began using the techniques in this chapter to ensure my health.

Despite my commitment to manifesting my health, I have gained enough wisdom to know better than to struggle against the ocean. There may or may not be a greater plan that this is all adding up to, but there definitely are situations that have developed with the full force of cause and effect behind them. The creative momentum of those situations is so powerful that to go against them means to fight the ocean. No one has ever won that battle.

I choose to believe that each of us has a responsibility to chart a course for ourselves in life. We must intend something, but we must not cling to anything.

I have made an art of doing just that. A combination of learning to create the conditions we believe will produce satisfaction and learning how to be happy under any conditions is the art. Let us focus first on creating the conditions for happiness, since it is probably what your mind hungers for more, though your soul will find far more satisfaction in later chapters in which we will look more closely at unconditional happiness, the true core of being bliss.

Living from Miracle to Miracle

I spent 1999 living in Bali, Indonesia. I went there because I wanted to live in a beautiful, tropical place that was so inexpensive that I could take modest savings with me and still be able to stay a year without working a job. I had not yet reached a point in my spiritual development where I was able to support myself through spiritual work, such as channeling, teaching ecstatic dance, or doing energy healing sessions.

While I was living in Bali I had the chance to dedicate much of my time to each of those pursuits. My ability to channel greatly expanded. I taught spiritual dance in a number of venues and even had the chance to perform it before hundreds of captivated Indonesians and westerners. And I came to a much deeper understanding of what was happening within energy healing in light of the new experiences I was having with channeling.

It was a miraculous time and I am grateful to myself for having given myself the chance to experience that. One of the most fortunate parts of the experience was being given a book by my next door neighbor titled *Conversations with Raj*. It is the story of a trance channel on the brink of enlightenment whose spiritual guide is trying to help him cross that final bridge. The guide says basically, "Remain in contact with me as much as possible. Maintain a field of peace within you and keep clarifying your intentions."

The channel of course is concerned about paying his rent and providing for his family who don't understand his sitting in meditation all day, day after day, month after month. They want him to get up and see to getting some clients through the door so money flows in. The phone is about to be turned off and the man goes to the guide and says, "Don't you think we should be a bit more balanced in our approach to this. I have responsibilities, you know." And Raj still keeps saying, "Focus on me. Stay in the field. Clarify your intentions."

Well the book never really says what happens to the man, or at least I have forgotten if it did. But I can tell you what happened to me when I applied Raj's guidance to my own life. Miracles.

You see, my calculations were way off. I had thought Bali was going to be cheap living and I could stay a year just off the money I made from selling my furniture and collecting the vacation pay from my last job before I left San Francisco. In actuality, I ran out of money after only 4 months.

I had an open ticket with up to a year I could stay, but decided that I was going home after 4 months because I had lived so lavishly that I was broke. So I reserved a seat on a flight leaving on a Tuesday. That Thursday I went to my friends and told them I was leaving so I wanted to get together with all of them that weekend for a party. One of my friends said, "You aren't leaving."

I said, "Well I have no money left and as a foreigner I can't get a job here in Indonesia, so I've got to go home now and make a new start back in America."

Again she insisted, "You aren't leaving."

For about a day I was disappointed by the idea of going home after such a short trip, but I remembered Raj's guidance to remain peaceful at all times. I did my channeling each day, as well as my meditation practice, and stayed focused on my desire to live in "paradise" for a year. I began and ended each meditation or channeling session with images of myself joyfully walking along the paths through the rice fields, the sun beaming down and a smile on my face. Or maybe I would be sitting on someone's veranda overlooking the fields, laughing as we sipped afternoon tea.

I filled my heart with joy each time I saw these scenes, thus empowering the vision as a joyful outcome. I had been told by Joliet, a guide I was channeling, that I must always remember that the product will match the process that created it. If I wanted the realization of the visualizations to result in joy, I had to be joyful while visualizing them. Otherwise I might get the picture of happiness, but not the experience of it. Does that sound like anything you're familiar with?

Anyway, I did what the guides were instructing me to do. The day after I announced my departure I was invited to a party at a spiritual retreat center out in Tabanan regency, where there are few westerners. I didn't want to leave Bali without having been to Tabanan so I accepted the invitation.

At the party I met a woman who I really clicked with. We had a great time talking and by the end she invited me to come visit with her at her home near Ubud. I was also living near Ubud and wanted to accept, but I told her it would have to be soon since I was leaving on Tuesday and it was now Saturday night.

She said emphatically, "You aren't leaving."

I told her about my financial situation, never for a moment feeling any lack in my circumstances, simply stating the truth of the matter.

She said that I should come with her to her workplace on Monday and meet her boss who she was sure would hire me to sell real estate to tourists. I explained that I had never sold anything in my life and knew nothing about real estate, least of all in a foreign country. Also, my business visa was expiring and I didn't have a work visa.

Again, she insisted that none of this would be a problem. And she was right. That Monday I did go with her to her workplace down in Sanur, I was offered a job, and her boss advanced me the money I needed to pay my rent and extend my existing visa by another month. I cancelled my plane reservations and settled back into my life in paradise.

It turned out I wasn't at all happy with selling real estate so I quit after just 9 days, but in those 9 days I made enough sales to earn the money to remain in Indonesia another month. Happy to be once more gainfully unemployed, I returned my full attention to my spiritual study and practice.

At the end of that month, I had again run out of money and so booked another flight out. I went to my friends again and told them I was leaving. Again the response was, yeah, yeah, right. And again I was invited to a party, this one at a beautiful home in Sayan, not far from where I lived.

At the party I entered a wonderful conversation with a man named Steven. He enjoyed my positive outlook and said he had watched me from the time I arrived at the party and noticed how I engaged each person I spoke with from a truly intimate and heartfelt space. He said that his ex-wife had also had a way of making each person at a party feel as if they were the only person in the room while she was talking to them, and that he had never appreciated that talent in her until he had lost her.

We talked for a long time then I said I should continue to meet some of the other guests. As I was leaving the party Steven stopped me again and said that he had been told that I was about to leave the island. I explained that I was out of money and so it was time for me to go home so that I would be able to work and earn a living.

He said that he had been intrigued by my explanations of the spiritual work I did, particularly that I taught spiritual dance, and wanted to know if I had ever thought about creating events. I informed him that I had been creating sacred arts events for small groups for years, but mostly just word of mouth affairs among an extended circle of friends.

It turned out that Steven was a successful businessman who was trying to make a life transition into sacred arts work but didn't really know how. He had ample funds to support any venture, but no direction in clarifying where to begin. I had lots of experience with content development for sacred arts events, but had never had enough funds to do anything at a truly professional scale.

We made plans to meet for lunch and within the week I was working with Steven to create what turned out to be a standing room only success. And he advanced me the money I needed to extend my visa another month and paid me a fee for my consulting services that was just enough for me to live in Bali another 2 months.

I think you see the pattern by now. Month by month, I was kept in Bali. When it finally came time for me to actually leave I tried to get friends together for a going away party but no one would come. They had started thinking it was my thing to just say I was leaving so everyone would throw parties for me!

I share this experience with you to demonstrate just how effective this simple formula is: 1) cultivate inner peace, whether through channeling, meditation, prayer, nature walks, whatever works for you; and 2) clarify your intentions.

As my spirit guide Joliet instructed, it is also important to add the emotion of joy to your visualizations of intent. If that seems impossible, just think of it as adding a halo of light around the visualization and let yourself think about how you will feel when the envisioned image comes into reality. If that thought doesn't arouse joy in you, you need to get another vision anyway.

I was able to stay in Bali for the amount of time I had first intended, but the manner in which I stayed was nothing I had imagined. I could not possibly have planned anything as miraculous as what occurred. Spirit was able to reach me through so many people I didn't even know at the beginning of the trip and tossed in my lap several opportunities to do things I had tried hard to do for many years before without success. As soon as I dropped the "efforting" and just surrendered to peace, while maintaining clarity about what I wanted to manifest, it all came to find me.

So am I saying you have to move to a tropical land of plenty in order to have life flowing your way? No.

After Bali I moved to New York City. Yes, from Bali to New York is a big transition. But it was where my inner guidance had indicated the most expansive spiritual growth lay for me at that time, and I go where I am sent.

When I arrived in New York I had very little money left and no real clarity about what I was going to do for work. A week after I got there I went to visit a friend from Bali who lived on the Upper West Side of Manhattan. We had a wonderful dinner and it got very late. She had a guest room so I stayed with her instead of making the two hour trip out to where I was staying in Queens.

The next morning she invited me to visit her at work. She said she had told her co-workers about me and they would probably enjoy meeting me. I had breakfast then walked over to the magnet school where she worked. I spent 3 hours chatting with various co-workers of hers, including the over-stretched guidance counselor, the principal, and the gym teacher who was also experimenting with dance classes in the new dance studio they had built. By the time I left I had been offered a job as a guidance counselor at the school who would be in charge of building up a dance therapy program for the children!

Of course, I was in no place to accept such an offer. I had only been in the country a week and hadn't even begun clarifying what my intentions for work were. But one thing became clear, the momentum of my spiritual practices was still unfolding so I needed to get focused on clarifying something right away. I didn't want to accept or turn down their offer before surveying my options.

The following work day I set an appointment at a placement agency and went to look for a job. I didn't expect or want to actually find a job. I just wanted to talk to a professional about my skills and abilities and get feedback on my appropriateness for various jobs.

It was fun getting dressed up in business attire and heading into Manhattan to meet with the recruiter. Imagine my shock when the maniac sent me out on two interviews that very week, both of which resulted in job offers. The first offer was for three times the highest salary I had ever made before and the second was even more attractive – and I wasn't even trying to actually land a job!

I decided I needed to get out of New York. I needed to sort out my goals and the energy was just moving too aggressively there for me. I was in a vulnerable internal space, having opened a great deal in the preceding two years, and I needed to be someplace where no demands were placed on me, even by me. I needed to be somewhere I knew I could not stay so there would be no pressure to make life decisions while I cleared my head.

Fortunately my eldest sister owned a large home near a lake in the woods of Maryland and the entire household left for work and school each day, leaving the house empty. I begged her to let me come stay in her guest room for a few weeks and she convinced her husband to agree.

It was just what I needed. I only regret that I didn't stay longer, but after a month I started feeling like a freeloader so I decided to head back to New York and look for work.

By then I had the clarity that none of the jobs I had been offered were right for me. The guidance position would be too emotionally demanding. The sales positions were in a field completely uninteresting to me. Meanwhile the tech bubble was just beginning to burst and there was a great deal of uncertainty in the air.

After a few months, which included a miserable experience temping at a media firm, I accepted a job selling computer classes. Although thankfully I excelled in the position, I quickly realized once more that I hate sales. My manager didn't want to lose me so he let me pick a different job at the company. I decided to teach the classes instead of selling them. That lasted another month. Within those two months I not only made enough money to move into a very nice rented room in Manhattan, but learned work skills that would later prove invaluable.

The next transition was into another temp agency. I felt bad about being such a flake up until then and decided that if I wasn't clear enough within myself to be able to keep any long-term commitments then I shouldn't make any. Temping seemed like the logical answer to bring in money in a very fluid arrangement, so I went back to that.

Just my luck, I got hired to do a position at the United Way where they ask all temps to sign a contract to stay a pre-agreed amount of time. My contract was set to end on Friday, December 15, ten days before Christmas. Had I thought ahead I never would have accepted the assignment. Who hires anyone at Christmas time? I would be unemployed until mid-January at least. Fortunately I did not think ahead so my mind did not have a chance to limit me to only what it could conceive. And the universe had bigger plans for me, miraculous plans.

During the three months I was at the United Way I continued to practice the manifestation techniques I had learned in Bali. I continued to spend most of my free time in meditation and to focus my attention primarily upon clarifying just what it was the image of my happiness would look like, particularly within the arena of work.

I had figured out that I wanted to do something in social services that involved helping people integrate into society. I myself had been an outsider throughout so much of my life that I knew the pain of alienation and wanted to spare others that same suffering. I thought when I set the intention that it would probably mean working with new immigrants to the United States, but all my inquiries into groups doing that work led to dead-ends.

I realized I was making the mistake of letting my intellect try to take over the goal made by my intuition and use its planning skills to attempt to manifest the goal. That is a big no-no when it comes to manifesting happy outcomes. The intellect can't even conceive of miracles so how could it possibly figure out a way to make them manifest? If we only get out of the way long enough to let intuition conceive of the greatest possible goal, but not long enough to let it achieve it, we will just face one frustration after another.

So I dropped back into the field of expectancy and turned it all back over to Spirit. Having maintained my inner peace while engaging in self-inquiry, I had successfully tapped into the wisdom of Spirit and seen Its highest vision for that phase in my life. I now had the clarity of intent I had been missing. All that was left was patience, positive expectation and continued focus.

As stated earlier, my job was ending on Friday December 15th. On Monday the 11th, I went out for a late dinner after a meditation class with some other students. At the dinner someone asked me, "Isn't your job ending soon?"

I confirmed. They asked what I was going to do next. I said I didn't know. Then I was asked what I had applied to. I said I hadn't applied to any jobs. They asked if I had savings to wait for the perfect job. I said I didn't have January's rent. The table fell silent.

Finally the silence was broken by Michael, who had invited me to join the meditation group. "Don't you think you should be looking for a job?" he asked.

I thought for a moment then responded, "Actually, when you put it like that, it does sound like I should be looking for a job, but for some reason I just haven't felt like it."

That was the end of the conversation. I imagine they gave up on trying to reason with an obvious fool.

Two days later, as I was sitting around after lunch with no work to do, it occurred to me that maybe it was time for me to look for a job, or at least to announce my general intentions to the Universe through the ritual act of applying for a job. So I went on the internet and pulled up some job listings.

I found one that seemed to describe just what I was looking for. It said something about helping people return to work, which is a very important part of being integrated into our society. The listing was a month old so I figured it must be filled already, but the point wasn't to get a job, just to announce to the Universe what kind to send me. Ever prepared, I pulled out my floppy disk with my resume on it and updated it swiftly with my current temp work.

I got a call at home that evening. It was the program director asking me in for an interview the following day. I went in to interview and it went well. On the way out to the elevator the Assistant Director told me they were going to make me an offer and that I should only accept after insisting on more money than whatever human resources offered. By the time I got back to the United Way my supervisor there told me someone had just called her to check my references and she had given me a glowing review. An hour later someone from human resources called to make the offer and asked if I could start work the following day. I apologized that I could not because I still had a commitment to my temp job for one more day, but agreed to start the following Monday, December 18 - for $4,000 more than their original offer (which happened to be the highest salary I had ever earned to begin with!).

So I ended one job on a Friday and started the next on the following Monday. And I got my first paycheck just in time to pay January's rent.

Breaking it Down to its Parts

Okay. Enough example. Let us focus more clearly now on just what it is you do to make this work for you.

The essence of this recipe really is just 2 ingredients with a little flavor thrown in. The ingredients are 1) mental and emotional peace and 2) a clear image of what you want to manifest. The flavor is that the image must produce a feeling of joy. That is also how you test to see that you have successfully clarified your intentions.

Peace

The development of peace of mind can take many forms. In the third section on Tools and Techniques you will find many practices you can do towards this end. But if you have made it this far in life, you must already have something you already do that gives you some degree of peace even in the midst of upheaval. Maybe it's taking a walk in the woods, playing with a dog, enjoying a hot bath, or an exhilarating game of neighborhood volleyball. Whatever it is, make time to do it and fully immerse yourself in the experience without mental dialog about whatever problem you are facing elsewhere in life.

Once you touch it, don't waste the experience on a night of carousing with buddies and gal friends. Don't go for drinks to celebrate a moment of freedom from anxiety. Instead go straight to your room and get to work clarifying your intentions. It is only from within a field of peace that you can discover the joy-filled visions of Spirit and choose goals that will lead you in joy.

Goal Clarification

The process of goal clarification can take a while, as it did for me when I relocated to New York, or can be instantaneous. It often moves in a spiral process. You use the technique to manifest one intention. You experience the result as something less than what you had hoped for, but probably a movement in the right direction. You create a new vision with greater self-understanding. And so on. You keep coming back to the same issue, but are a little closer to the center of it on each revolution.

In order for the field of universal abundance, an aspect of your Divine nature, to shine through your vision, the vision must be in alignment with that light. The more deeply you are connected with the field of peace when you form your goals, the more likely the vision is coming from Spirit. Also, make sure you get a "Yes" answer to each of the following questions when you examine your vision: Is the vision in alignment with your best possible future? Does it benefit both you and others? Does it allow others freedom? Does the thought of it manifesting fill you with a sense of peace and fulfillment? Does the vision reflect your equality with others instead of your superiority? If you get a "No" to any of these questions, clarify your vision some more.

Empowerment

Empowering the vision of the desired outcome with the emotion of joy will make the spiral process much shorter. The details of how the image manifests are not important. What is important is that the result leads to joy. You use the image to evoke the emotion, then drop the image completely. Do not be attached to images.

Another Perspective

There is another way of looking at this process that is also helpful. You can also think of it as a formula of Attention, Choice, Empowerment, and Surrender, all operating within a spiral of creation. There are two levels within this spiral process. There is the level of seated manifestation sessions in which you create the internal experience. And there is the level of lived experience in which you apply the technique in the flow of life to seize opportunities for the manifestation of the happy goal.

The Inner Level

At the inner manifestation level, seated practice sessions, attention is to the present moment where peace lies. The thought of peace is insufficient. For the method to work you must have the experience of peace and all experience is had within the present. Past "experience" is actually just a memory, a type of thought. Future "experience" is really a hope, another type of thought. True experience is not a thought and is always happening right now. So you sit and pay attention to your experience right here and now. In doing this, you uncover your inner peace.

The choice made is whatever is intended. When you are clarifying your intentions you are really clarifying choices. You recognize your responsibility and power to create whatever exists in your life and you embrace that responsibility by exercising your right to choose.

The empowerment is the emotion of joy that is applied to the process. You are an ecstatic creator, not a reluctant one, wishing someone would save you from yourself and you could just go back to sleep. You are excited about what you are creating and enjoy the creative act itself.

And the surrender is letting go of the demand that the outcome look exactly like the image, understanding that the image is just a tool. This last one is often hardest for people. But we must not limit the miracles that manifest in our lives to only what the intellect can conceive. Surrender creates space in which Spirit can work. So our seated manifestation session always ends with the disclaimer, "This or something better, Thy will be done." I often like to say it, "Thy will be mine" to emphasize even more strongly that I intend to cooperate with the movement of the great ocean.

The Outer Level

In the realm of lived experience, as you get up from your seat and move out into the world, these four points take a slightly different form. Attention is now about alertness. It is still attention to the present moment, but the focus is more on awareness of what is happening within and around you in the flow of life so that when the opportunity to realize your goal presents itself you are ready to act.

Choice is involved in that you must act with discernment. That does not mean being judgmental, clamping your mind around everything you see like an iron vise. There is not the passion of judgment. There is no attachment, no demand, no rejection, but there is a clear choice that is made in terms of which decision in that moment moves you closer to the goal and which does not. You do not waste the opportunities of life. You are alert and act with decisiveness.

Empowerment is very much the same as in the seated manifestation practice. You take a happy attitude towards life and expect the best to happen. Think of your life as moving from miracle to miracle, or perhaps from blessing to blessing if you aren't the excitable type. Frame the story of your life anew as one that tells the tale of a happy person whose life flows smoothly and to whom good things come in the most delightful ways. Look at every situation, no matter how unfavorable it appears on the surface, as some part of a developing blessing that may or may not be fully comprehensible for your intellect yet.

Surrender in daily life means leaving some space there. How is Spirit going to bless you in unexpected ways if every minute of your life conforms to an established routine? Even if you have a very demanding schedule with many responsibilities to others, that is no excuse for shirking your responsibilities to yourself. This world needs you in your joy. There are enough morose, angry, would-be do-gooders out there martyring themselves and ruining everything for all of us. Humanity doesn't need you in that club.

Take a walk without a destination and let your inner guidance tell you which direction to start in, which way to turn at each intersection, and when it is time to head home. And be sure you make your way home in the same manner, not trying to take the shortest route but rather the one Spirit is sending you along. No time for a walk? Then take the long way home from work some days and be willing to stop anywhere that seems to pull you towards it.

The spiral will cause you to keep coming back to the same lessons again and again, but that is so that you get to learn how to make a more expansive choice. Think bigger. You are far more than who you think you are. And yet, you do not exist at all as who you think you are.

Above all, remember always step one – be attentive. Remain alert, constantly listening for the whisper of your inner voice and sensing for some movement within your spiritual heart. Let your field of awareness be broad enough to take in both your outer experience (usually more like your thoughts about your outer experience) and your inner experience. It may take practice if you are used to being narrowly focused, but you can expand the scope of your viewing lens if you fully intend to.

The Final Word on Choice vs. Determinism

Buddhism says there is no ultimate aim pursued by the infinite "luminous emptiness" nor any personality trait to it beyond pure awareness itself. The law of our lives is simply cause and effect. We should do good because cause and effect makes it in our best interest to do good. Doing good benefits both self and others, therefore it is advisable. We do not seek to please a God and we do not face a pre-determined end to human existence. Various schools of Buddhism have slightly different teachings, but for the most part one can describe it this way.

Most other religions say there is plan for all of life and that it is good. Often they go further to say we will be punished by the planner if we don't do good, but the threatening part doesn't resonate with my sense of truth at all.

It makes sense to me that there is some order to what is unfolding in all these galaxies which could simply be based on momentum created by all choices made. No guiding agenda. No grand finale. But while there may be no intrinsic nature to the stillness beneath it all and so no planning involved at that level, the manifestation has some clearly definable characteristics.

What I see is that the overwhelming movement of life is that of goodness. Look at the incredible generosity of nature, for example – at how we have been given life and a world of great beauty that supports that life. Look at all the love flowing in the world.

Now maybe it's still just cause and effect. Maybe there is a basic goodness to life because, contrary to what the media would have you believe, there is just more good happening in the world than bad. Right now, there are more people actively feeling love for someone than feeling hate. There are more people doing a good deed for someone than ripping someone off. There are more people, right now, saying a prayer for peace than praying for war.

It seems that the basic experience of human life is one that includes far more joy, peacefulness, and love than the reverse. It just isn't the dominant story our media gives us to explain our lives, so it's easy to miss. Moment by moment, we are creating a future that reflects who we truly are and our nature really is essentially good. In time, that dominant story will get more and more of a leg up regardless of whether there is a master plan.

There doesn't have to be an organizing mind with a single intent that is destined to save us from ourselves in order for this adventure to turn out quite well. If you have enough of the parts working with the same benevolent intent, then there is a natural order and effectiveness that comes through. Perhaps this "reality" is a coherent system. Apply joyful intent from enough points of influence and the outcome is a joyful expression of our potential.

It certainly is a more joyful life from a personal viewpoint when we choose to manifest joyful situations for ourselves and others. Moreover, when we make choices that flow with the momentum of all the goodness unfolding in the universe (particularly at the angelic levels filled with extremely powerful co-creators) we get to ride a mighty current. We don't have to make the journey solely based on our own energy.

When we choose to do harm, we go it alone. Even what support we can find for our selfish aims is dubious. Our compatriots are as likely to eat us as aid us. We wind up struggling unto exhaustion, trying to shape life according to our isolated will alone, without even the assistance of our own souls.

Whether as an impersonal result of the momentum of the goodness that is being thought, spoken and done in the universe or as the loving intent of a single conscious planner, it appears Life wants to bless us. It is in Its nature to be generous.

The rules for tapping into all the abundance waiting for us are simple because it was meant to be easy. Let Life love you. Choose the most loving images for yourself and empower them with the most joyful emotions. Trust the basic flow of life to not exclude you from its natural journey into joy. Remain alert and seize the chance to exercise your creative choice whenever it comes. Be peace. Be joy. Be bliss.

Try This for Three Days:

Every hour on the hour (or as close as you can get) ask yourself the following question:

"What do I want right now?"

Then visualize yourself doing whatever that is. As you envision it, fill yourself with a feeling of joy and vigor. If you are able, immediately do whatever it was you envisioned and observe whether you actually do feel joy and enthusiasm while doing it.

At the end of the day, take a few minutes to reflect on the envisioned joys of each hour. Which ones did you act upon? What affected the choice to act or just think about the desire? How difficult or easy was it to know what you wanted at any given moment? How often did your choices lead to an experience that matched your expectations? Were your desires primarily things you wanted to be, to do, or to have?

What emotions came up for you during the process? Were there any issues of worthiness or permission or did you feel quite comfortable with the idea of getting, being or doing whatever you wanted throughout the day? Was there any way for you to tell which wants were coming from the level of your ego self and which were coming from Spirit?

I suggest you make this reflection process a written one. If you started the journal recommended in the introduction, use that. If you skipped the introduction or decided not to start a journal to record this growth process, a formal journal for this exercise isn't necessary (though it will be beneficial if you want to be able to look back on this experiment later). Even just writing down a few notes on scrap paper will help you to focus your thoughts and prevent you from wandering off into habitual thinking in the middle of the exercise. It should only take about 5 minutes if you stay focused on the task at hand.

Try it for 3 days. See what it's like for you to directly engage the process of envisioning your desires as already fulfilled then acting from that place of joy.

2 LOVE IN ACTION

"Lord, make me an instrument of Thy peace." - *St. Francis of Assisi*

In the first chapter we talked about how you create the conditions you want in life and the happiness that goes with that satisfaction. This is useful, and it's probably what you want to learn about most, but it is not the only form of happiness. Now that I have hopefully helped you develop some peace of mind in that regard, let me speak to another part of you.

You now know how to manifest whatever you want whenever you want, though you may still need more practice before you feel a sense of mastery. Hopefully you can now be secure enough to stop grasping after anything or running from anything. Therefore, enough indulging that scheming intellect of yours. I know you have one; we all do. Please stop for a moment, close your eyes, and turn inward to find the part of yourself connecting you to wisdom and peace.

The second key to happiness is service to others. Let yourself be a pathway for healing, love and peace moving out into this world. Instead of pursuing your happiness by endlessly manifesting favorable conditions, think more about supporting the happiness of others and live in quiet confidence regarding your own well-being. We are all interconnected, fellow travelers in this universe. Whenever you help another you are ultimately helping a part of yourself, and whether consciously or not, you will experience the results of that service sooner or later.

Once you know how to manifest whatever you need whenever you need it, to live as if you were desperate would undermine your powers to manifest, for such behavior creates more of itself. You will manifest situations reflecting lack if you see yourself as lacking something. Instead rest in your wholeness and from that place of abundance look out to see what you can do for this world.

This altruistic action will not come from grasping. It will not reflect a desperate need to be of use. It will be natural and easy. It will be the Truth of unconditional love naturally unfolding in this world through you.

Do not look at the world for what you can get. Look for the opportunities to give. Rest in gratitude for all you have and for your ability to manifest whatever you need. Turn your conscious intent towards images of yourself spreading blessings. Be alert. Act with enthusiasm whenever you perceive a chance to fulfill some need of others, but do not grasp after such chances either. Reach towards nothing, but intend, allow, and rejoice in all situations.

Selflessness

Selflessness is essential to happiness, but what is selflessness? Does that mean that you are nothing and that everyone else is more important than you? The word can be used that way, but really that is not the true meaning of selflessness, not in a spiritual context.

Selflessness means to awaken to the true unity of all beings. When you realize that you are one with everyone you meet, suddenly it makes no sense to go on clinging to yourself or disregarding them. They are you. Their happiness is not more important than yours – it is yours!

This is the truth, but you may or may not be experiencing it consciously. You may not be in touch with your deepest feelings and responses, but I promise you that there within you is the awareness of an unseverable connection between you and every other living being. If you don't already experience this, doing the emotional clearing exercises in the third section will make it easier for you to experience more of yourself and then you will know from experience that what I am saying is true.

Years ago I was walking down the streets of New York City. It was a cold winter night and I was tired after a long day working as an administrative temp at a media firm filled with unhappy, cynical people. As I hurried towards the subway, huddled against the wind to try to protect my neck and chest from the chill, I saw a homeless man lying on the ground. He too was huddled against the cold, but had one arm stuck out holding a paper cup for donations.

As I passed him I heard him whimpering. He was crying and saying, "Please. Please. Please help. Somebody. Anything."

Continuing at my brisk pace, I thought of how much money I had on me. I had not received my first paycheck yet and hadn't worked for American money in over a year. I had to be able to get to and from work until I was paid and had to be able to eat lunch as well. What could I spare for this man? My mental calculations said, "Nothing. You'll be lucky if you don't need to borrow money yourself before the week is out."

Thankfully, my spiritual self took over my body. Before I knew what was happening I had stopped dead in my tracks and started back towards the man, who was now silent. I reached in my bag and pulled out the $3 I had on me and stooped down towards him. I thought I was going to watch myself put the last of my cash in his cup, but instead an awareness dawned within me that more than the money, this man needed to be loved and he needed to feel that love in his flesh. I watched in awe as my hand reached towards his and carefully tucked the small wad of bills between the cup and his hand, being careful to press one finger into his soft flesh as it did so.

"Here you go," I heard my mouth say, as I quickly turned and started back down the street towards my train.

Before I could reach the subway entrance I was hit by a wave of energy that came rushing down the street behind me. It was as if I was swept up in the arms of God. I was filled and lifted and carried forward as a wave within a vast ocean of love. Perhaps the man had looked at me with loving gratitude, or perhaps it was not directly from him. I don't know. I only know that I was adrift in that ocean of love, joy, and peace all the way home. The subway was a heavenly realm filled with angels and I was one with it all.

Of course, that meddlesome intellect of mine was still busy working in the background and so at some point it occurred to me that the man was unclean and that I had touched him. I could not resist wiping my finger on my pant leg, and as I did I felt my mental comfort grow and the energy of bliss diminish. Just as I had performed an act of connectedness on the street, I had just performed one that confirmed a belief in separation. Fortunately, the latter was not strong enough to completely obliterate the former, and so it was still a truly blissful ride home.

There is only one of us. There is only one of us! Did you hear the good news? There is only one of us.

A few days ago I was sitting on my meditation cushion experimenting with an energy meditation of the Shingon Buddhist tradition from which Reiki originates. In the method you breathe in the clear light of universal life force energy through the crown chakra at the top of the head, sending it down into the dan tien below the belly button. Then as you breathe out you radiate that purifying, loving energy in all directions at once, sending it out to heal all the world. You give it all away.

I was amused to watch myself doing this meditation. That self-obsessed intellect of mine was acting up again. I noticed my resistance to breathing out the energy. I was feeling drained after a 3 hour healing session earlier that day followed by several hours of intense research and wanted to keep the energy for myself.

Being the good student I am, I did the meditation according to instructions despite my inner resistance. After 10 minutes I decided I'd had enough so I stopped. A split second later a flood of energy I would characterize as energizing and warmly affectionate rushed into me from all directions at once. It was as if the tide I sent out had turned back on me.

I realized then that the meditation did not involve me bringing in Divine energy so that I could channel it into physical reality as a gift to others. It was me focusing Divine energy within the physical aspect of myself and nothing more. I am the world. No, not my ego, not my intellect, not this body and identity history – that is all separate and limited and doomed to die. But ME. The real me is one with all that truly exists and is beyond the veils of this illusion.

Each time I sent energy "out" I was really sending it "around," just to a different part of myself. But since all the parts are really connected by a massive cosmic circulatory system, what was sent elsewhere eventually had to come flowing back to its starting place. I was blessed in that higher wisdom saw fit to send me a teaching through the experience so that I had instant karma. The time between the sending and receiving was greatly shortened so that my intellect could perceive the connection between events clearly.

Another thing you may be learning from these experiences I am sharing with you is that I am very much on the road, just as you are. I often experience a view of reality that understands the true unity of all things, but not always. It is an ongoing process of unlearning the illusion of separation that I have been brainwashed into calling "reality" all my life.

Even still, if I go to certain sorts of movies or catch a glimpse of TV somewhere, the propaganda starts working at me again. For weeks after I see some movies I have their images swimming around in my head, emerging into consciousness whenever they feel like it with absolutely no invitation from me.

Rarely are they images that reflect the beauty and majesty of our collective lives. There is an awful lot of violence in our society's "entertainment" and that is not the result that I want my thoughts to cause, so I find other past-times. Be deliberate about what you expose your mind to. You are highly impressionable.

Embracing a Higher Mind

If you have an illusion that you are in charge of your mind, I've got news for you, you're not. Watch your mind sometime and see. Watch how with no prompting from you whatsoever your thoughts move from this, to that, to the next thing. Who is making this thought follow that one? Who or what is running this show?

It is inertia. You are not a "you" so much as a collection of habitual responses. For instance, you sit in meditation, ready to watch the mind according to meditation instruction. There is a contraction in a leg muscle. Your mind interprets pain. You imagine a story of injury. You feel worry or anger or fear. And so on.

But what happened? A muscle contracted, as muscles tend to periodically do. It meant nothing, but now you are having an experience of troubling emotions and have interrupted your meditation for it. The mind has a strong habit of interrupting meditations, and you have indulged it. Who is in charge of that mind of yours?

This habit pattern of "you" has been indoctrinated to believe that it is a solid self whose existence must be defended and whose interests must be promoted. Self-seeking and self-protection are the two strongest habits in your system, and they are directly opposed to one of the primary sources of happiness in life, which is selflessness. Hence your dilemma.

I hope you will take a look at your mind for yourself to see that what I am describing is true so that real understanding will emerge within you. If you don't look to see for yourself, maybe you believe me, maybe you don't, but either way you won't get to actually KNOW. If not now, at least when you get to the end of this chapter, please stop a moment to take this voyage of self-discovery.

When you look you will see, "Yes, that is what is going on in my experience. There is no "me" there, only a flow of sensations, perceptions, thoughts, emotions, and so on. This flow moves about constantly and jumps from here to there reactively without any peace in sight." Now you know. Then what?

I am trying to convince you of something that I know your intellect will resist, but I try anyway because I believe it is the key to your happiness that you understand this, and I want you to be happy. This part of Myself is quite happy much of the time, because I already know this, but that part of Myself that is perceiving through *your* life experience may be still learning to be happy under adverse conditions. I want all of me to be as happy as possible as much as possible, so I am working very hard here at finding a way to get through the shield of your intellect and convince it to recognize it isn't in complete control anyway so why not give up the illusion of control and let something more effective take over?

And here is the crux of the matter. You cannot surrender your selfishness without something to surrender it to. You cannot simply choose to disappear. Not even a suicidal person really does that. I know because as I mentioned in the introduction I attempted suicide many times in my youth. Always there is still some hope that emerges in the final moments when it seems you are really about to disappear. No matter how we suffer, we always wish to continue in some form, albeit one that is free of suffering.

So you will not be able to just stop the madness within you that your intellect is supposedly directing effectively, which you have now discovered is really just chaos, unless you find something else to put in charge. The good news is, something else is already running much of your life.

Who is it that makes you breathe? Hold your breath for five minutes, don't breathe. Whoops. What happened? Try again. What is it that forces you to breathe when your mind has decided clearly that it intends not to breathe? Your body? Is it your body that is in control then? All right, grow 3 inches taller. Heal that scrape on your knee. Fly.

There is something running this show that makes flowers grow, wounds heal, and babies radiate peace and joy through their very presence. I call it the All-pervading Light and Love, Spirit, the luminous emptiness, God for short – though by "God" I don't mean a human image sitting somewhere casting judgments.

My God has no distinct image and is unconditional in Its generosity. How could It not be? All that It made It made out of Itself and It continues to pervade all that It created. We are It. It is Us. And We love Our Self unconditionally.

Surrender to that. Let that which creates life guide life. Place yourself solidly in the middle of the flow of the great ocean and let it carry you where it will. Do not go it alone within the great ocean, for no one is safe alone in the face of such overwhelming magnitude. It is not a desire to control you that makes this so. It is simply the nature of the situation. Life is vast, so vast that your isolated intellect, even if you are an Einstein, is incapable of managing everything that significantly impacts you. The good news is, there is a benevolent force that is quite capable and quite willing.

"Wait a minute," you may be thinking, "weren't you saying that there was no great planner with a great plan ready to save us from ourselves?"

Yes, and I am still saying that. We are the great planner and what We intend is the plan. Fortunately much of who We are is enlightened. It is cohesive, self-aware, peaceful, loving, incredibly powerful and tirelessly at work manifesting Our plans.

Whenever we do something to benefit others we act in harmony with that greater part of who we are. Sometimes the decision to benefit others comes from our Divine Self and sometimes it comes from a type of self-discipline and morality imposed by our small, separate self. Either way, service to others works in harmony with the type of decisions we make at the level of our identity that is beyond parts.

As I said before, I clearly note that there are distinct characteristics to what manifests at the highest level of reality we can perceive. There is a clear goodwill to what Life chooses for us. Sometimes it is hard to see with our limited perspective, but time usually reveals the benevolence hidden within even the most challenging life lessons.

We are responsible for what we create. At the individual level this responsibility takes the form of teachings from life. But at an ultimate level we are all connected and the experiences of all affect and inform the whole. The power and harmony within that Ultimate Whole, within God, makes It the best guide for the individual parts if we are to attempt to effortlessly create lives that match Its coherence, beauty, and joy. Successfully learning that means mastering the greatest lesson of them all.

By letting life work for you instead of trying to make life work, you will find many blessings come to you effortlessly. That is how I live. My life moves from blessing to blessing. I let it. I celebrate it, and I share it.

My individual mind is responsible for whatever it creates, but it can only see a few steps ahead. It often produces less than desirable results simply out of nearsightedness. Fortunately, I and many others have discovered a way to produce results that we will always be happy to accept. We don't use our minds! We have come to see that the wisest use of free-will is to choose to give it back! We have decided to make decisions from our greater, connected mind instead of our small, separate minds.

Each day when I wake up I make it clear to God that I have no intention of taking any of this upon myself. "You are the one that wanted all this diversity in life. Well here it is, this complicated vastness that I cannot possibly manage. So knock yourself out. Have fun. I'll just watch."

And I do. I watch God live this life and I have discovered something amazing about God. God is much smarter than me. And I am fairly smart, but God is much, much, much smarter.

God is also much kinder, more patient and much more generous. It doesn't matter to God whether a person is awake to their inner divinity or is acting unconsciously. God just gives blessings whenever It gets a chance to get in there and do so. God seems to particularly like blessing me, but it probably just appears that way from my viewpoint because I take such great joy in the blessings God gives <u>anyone.</u>

Oh yes, I make it *easy* for God. I want to be very happy so I make it really easy. I am always on the look-out for ways I can give God an opening into a situation. If I see a cashier with a frown on her face, I let God use my face to smile at her and use my voice to give her a kind word. I experience great joy when I feel God moving through me in this way. There is not a thought of getting something in return. The direct experience is reward enough. Sometimes there isn't any response on the person's face, but I can feel in my heart something opening and softening and I know God is in there. God always finds a way in if any party in a situation invites the Divine presence.

Praying for Others

Our prayers for others are essential to our own happiness. Whenever Spirit is moving through us it feels really good. It is impossible to not be happy while Spirit is working through you. Sometimes it may be a rush of energy that overcomes you like in the previous experiences I shared with you, but usually it is more subtle. Even in subtlety, it always feels really, really good to experience our oneness with Spirit.

Your prayers for others make a difference, both for that part of You that is reading this and for all the parts of You that you can reach out to as a result of making the choice to let Spirit heal the world through you. Let Spirit bring joy to all the parts of Itself through the particular identity continuum that is reading this and you will know double happiness.

A few months ago I was listening to Niki Haris sing "Someone Needs a Prayer," at a performance of the Agape Choir. As I listened I was transported back to a time years earlier when I had just returned from Bali and needed to stay with others until I could get a job and place of my own. For a couple of months I found myself staying in a household with many children, including two from other families who were in an informal daycare arrangement.

One of those children was a 5 year old boy I'll call Sam who had some emotional and intellectual retardation and so was slow to learn and rather disobedient. The caretakers didn't know how to take care of such a child, so the result was what I could easily identify as emotional abuse. I tried as best I could to bring this to the attention of his caretakers and encourage them to be more gentle and understanding, but it was to no avail. I then tried intervening whenever I saw abuse going on, defending him and comforting him quite openly. This only led to arguments and did not change the behavior.

One morning I woke up to hear someone yelling at the child whose mother had obviously just dropped him off minutes earlier. It was the last straw for me. I broke down crying, sobbing really, and prayed to God, "Why is this happening? Why can't I help? I cannot bear to watch this anymore, but I don't know what to do. Please help me. If I can't take him out of the darkness, please God, let me at least be a light for him in the darkness. Can't I at least be that? Please, please, please, God. Let me be a light for him in this darkness."

A few days later I came upon the children playing in the living room and was struck by an impulse to take Sam for a walk. I asked his caretaker if it would be all right then argued the strength of my intent (basically making it clear it wasn't really a request) when I met opposition. Finally I was given permission to take Sam out of the house. Sam sprung up with joy at the idea that he was going somewhere. He grabbed the little money he had and off we went.

Out on the street, I didn't really know where to take him. I felt to turn right out of the yard so we did. Then when we got to the first intersection I decided to ask Sam which way to go, left, right, or forward. He was nervous at first, not understanding someone asking him what he wanted and being willing to follow his direction. But after I made it clear we weren't going anywhere until he chose, he picked forward. At the next block I again asked him which way to go. Block by block, we took our walk. Finally he spotted a corner store and it quickly became clear he now had a destination. So we went to the store and he used his change to buy treats out of the quarter candy machines.

Returning from the store, as we got closer and closer to the house, I had this nagging feeling of inadequacy. I kept feeling like it wasn't enough. Sam had had fun, but there wasn't a shift. I wanted the shift. So I gave it another try. I offered to trade songs with him. I expected him not be willing to sing, but wanted to use the trade as an excuse for him to listen to me sing a song I had often sang to the delight of my nieces and nephews. He agreed to the song swap and I sang him "Happy Talk" from South Pacific.

When I was done I said, "Okay, now it's your turn. Are you ready to sing for me?" He nodded yes, and then he sang. And this is how he began:

"Carry a light, into the darkness. Carry a light. Carry a light...."

It was as if I had been hit with a bolt of friendly lightning. I was electrified with God's love and truly speechless. As he sang it, over and over, I heard the voice of God speaking to me. God was saying, "I have heard your prayers and I answer them. I always hear, and I always answer. I am in this situation."

There are prayers of thoughts, such as breathing life-force energy for the planet. There are prayers of words, like the one I said for little Sam. There are prayers of deeds, such as when I touched the hand of the beggar while giving him money. Whichever kind you decide to offer, someone needs your prayers today. Go and find them.

"Assuredly, I say to you, inasmuch as you did it to one of the least of these My brethren, you did it to Me." (Jesus the Christ, Matt. 25:40, *NKJ*)

Try This For 3 Days:

Tonglen is a traditional Buddhist meditation practice for developing compassion. When there is someone you care about who is sick or in despair and there is nothing you can directly do to help them, this is a wonderful practice for sending them blessings. It is also good to do for people you don't really like, even if they are doing quite well already. It will help you make peace with them within your heart.

Sit with your back supported in an upright position. As you breathe in, imagine that white light was flowing in with your breath, filling and permeating every corner of your being. As you breathe out, imagine that all that is conflicted, sorrowful, guilt-ridden, or heavy within you is released into the air around you where it is instantly converted into pure light. With each breath cycle, watch yourself grow more and more radiant as you become free of suffering and full of light. Do this until you feel like you are holding all the light you can comfortably contain.

Now begin to think about someone you love dearly, perhaps your mother. See her clearly in your mind. Imagine that you can see both her joys, represented by clarity around her, and her worries, shames and sorrows, represented by murky clouds around her.

As you breathe in, imagine that some of the cloudy matter was being drawn off her and flowing into you with your breath. As it enters your energy body it becomes pure light and you shine even more brightly. Then as you breathe out, send some of your pure, bright light out to her so that she also begins to shine more brightly.

Breathe in again and draw more of the clouds off her and into you. Breathe out again and send her more of your increasingly brilliant light. Do this until she is completely clear of clouds and shining brightly. You should feel full of energy and mentally peaceful when you are done.

Now repeat the process with someone you feel neutral about, perhaps a clerk you see sometimes at the local store. Then do the process a fourth time with someone you dislike. Each round should take just a few minutes so if you can sit for 15-20 minutes you can easily cover the various levels of intimacy you have with others. If you can't concentrate for that long, just do the exercise with yourself and someone you love for now and build up to the complete process over time.

There should be no grasping or trying to create a particular effect in anyone. Spend 3 days offering your compassion to those dear and not-so-dear with complete equanimity.

3 BEYOND CONDITIONS

So far we have looked at two sources of happiness in life, the joy of receiving and the joy of giving. Being able to create the life you want without struggle is wonderful. I want you to enjoy that type of happiness. It is also beautiful to uplift others and experience the joy of service. I want you to enjoy that fulfillment and high self-esteem as well, but what I want most for you is for you to know the kind of happiness that does not depend on anything outside yourself.

Here is the real story about happiness: The happiness that has the greatest value is the kind that doesn't depend on gaining or maintaining anything, whether for yourself or for someone else. It comes from a place of already feeling whole, intrinsically connected to the web of life, and it is unconditional.

It is a necessary part of conditions that they will change. Life is an ever moving flow. If you have been using the techniques found in the first chapter you've probably already seen yourself manifest sundry conditions that you thought would end your yearning. And for a time I am sure many of your "miracles" did bring you joy. Then you saw through them. It was really something slightly different you wanted. So then you manifested that. Closer to the mark, but still partial or fleeting. Back to work, and on it goes.

It is worthwhile to manifest favorable conditions in life. We want stability and sufficient comfort, beauty, and quiet in the place we live so that peace of mind is easier to achieve and we can focus more of our energy on other things. We want work that is meaningful so that we enjoy the passage of time in the day, not always reaching towards some distant moment when it is finally over and we can get back to "real" life. And we want loving relationships with other people, whether friends, lovers – whatever the relationship – that are emotionally intimate and filled with mutual goodwill and affection. This is a psychological need as a social animal. Babies will fail to thrive if not given enough loving touch, and you will slowly wither away too.

This chapter is by no means a refutation of the two that have come before it. As your naturally blissful self you will routinely manifest happy conditions for yourself and others, but the emphasis now is in learning not to make saviors out of our tools. You do not need to trade your obsession with elusive satisfactions for an obsession with attainable ones.

When you want something sincerely and see how it will support your peace of mind or bless another, manifest it. Simple. Do it and move on. But do not make a practice of searching the areas of your life for things in need of improvement. Do not become addicted to self-improvement. And certainly don't become obsessed with a mission to save the world. The greatest gifts you have to give come when you are moving from a place of inspiration, not compulsion.

At this point you are ready to focus your attention, intention and effort on a higher goal. In time this higher goal will take care of all the minor goals you have been manifesting favorable situations to handle.

The higher goal is this: Live as your highest possible self. Be Spirit living through a human life – yours.

This is the key to untouchable, dependable, utterly fulfilling happiness in human life. Live in complete oneness with your higher self and you will be living as a naturally blissful being who watches the ebb and flow of conditions with curiosity and amusement. Instead of finding it outside yourself, you will be the joy, peace and love you have been seeking in life.

Who Is This "Higher Self?"

Ultimately all terms we use to describe "The Ultimate All" are just concepts. We use the concepts because they help us talk about what is actually beyond words. The Truth can only be experienced and when it is experienced all conversation ceases.

Throughout this book we will use a certain system of dividing up the realm of Spirit so that you can work from where you are to get to where you want to be – living the experience that is beyond duality. Please keep in mind, however, that the system is a means to an ends and is in no way meant to be a description of the one way things must be described in order to be accurate. So long as we are using words, we are working with levels of truth, not the Truth itself. If you have a system of terminology that works better for you, substitute that. Don't get hung up on the words.

Within the system presented here, we will use the term "higher self" to indicate the particular aspect of Spirit that shines through your life experience whenever you allow it to. You can think of it as a localized experience of an infinite reality.

That said, in speaking of the higher self I am referring to what some people may call the soul or the individual connection to Spirit. Within the full spectrum of cosmic consciousness it is useful to consider various forms energy takes. There are numerous intermediate levels of differentiation we can think of between the Ultimate-Infinite-Unified-All – sometimes known as God – and the separate ego identity – also known as your personality.

Those beings we think of as guides, or in Buddhism as "deities," have a viewpoint of wholeness and act to help all the seemingly separate parts of their Self experience love, joy, and peace. Rather than thinking of them as beings, I find it most accurate to think of them as functions, and when I channel their guidance that is how they describe themselves. Some have the function of fostering peace, others motivating spiritual development, promoting health, many roles, but there is no delusion of being a solid, individual self.

Our human personalities, on the other hand, have little cohesiveness because they believe they really are separate. They only perceive their effect on others when it is direct and immediate. Your higher self is more cohesive than your personality, but it is probably not as cohesive as guide if you are still incarnating in a physical body. Your higher self is still expanding, moving towards "angel-consciousness" and ultimately "God-Consciousness." Still, your higher self has a sufficient level of unity consciousness to recognize its connection to Spirit. It can therefore allow you to experience the beauty, fulfillment and wisdom of that connection.

Your higher self is an aspect of who you are, in this lifetime and in all your lifetimes. It is a part of you that never fully incarnates. It is aware of its connectedness right now and has a far wider perspective than your personality self does. It is a tremendous source of guidance in life, both in terms of its ability to give you access to wisdom gained in all your lifetimes, and in its ability to connect you with the wisdom of angels, spiritual guides, and the "inner guru" or "holy spirit," the guiding principle of Spirit that is always there to lead us back into full awareness of the Truth.

As already stated, your higher self is living all of your lives (past, present and future) right now, but each of your separate identities within all those lives has free-will. Each one gets to choose where it directs its attention and how it decides its actions. You get to pick your own master.

When you decide to let your higher self guide your life, your personality gets to see this world with the eyes of Divinity. This greatly accelerates your development of wisdom, which in turn makes it even easier to experience the world as a reflection of Divine perfection. There is a wonderful snowball effect to every decision to allow Spirit to guide you through your higher self. Similarly, there is a reverberating effect to each decision to choose the ego as master, but the results aren't quite so pretty.

In the third section I will offer you many tools and techniques for strengthening your relationship with your higher self so that you can fully embody it with increasing frequency. For now I want to emphasize that this is the most useful goal you can set for yourself if you truly want to live in a state of bliss at all times. The most efficient way to move beyond the limitations of this reality is to see through them, and the vision of the higher self will allow you to do exactly that.

Signs along the way

A feeling of well-being is the easiest litmus test for whether you are living as your higher self. If you feel a sense of peaceful enjoyment, you are probably acting from your connection with your higher self. If you don't, you're off, so do something about that. Reconnect. Connect with your higher self again and again and you will be walking a life path of joy.

In joining with your higher self you will be bringing forth all the energies of Divine Love in your life. Your higher self is fully connected with Universal Love at all times.

Love opens and receives. It is a willingness to be touched and changed by something or someone. It is acceptance and embrace, without conditions. You surrender to your higher self and your higher self lives in constant surrender to Truth – to all that is, just as it is.

What we call love, joy, and peace are really just different ways we relate to true love when we are living as our higher selves. Within our world of duality in which ideas like "self" and "other" seem completely real, what we normally call love actually refers to Divine love directed outward; we are unconditionally open to the other and let Spirit love them through us. Joy is Divine love directed at the self; we accept ourselves and embrace all aspects of the life we have created, allowing ourselves to fully receive Spirit's love for us with gratitude and celebration. Peace is an unshakable connection to Divine love; we have faith in Spirit's love for us even in the midst of the most challenging situations.

Through the higher self we bring forth all the qualities of Divine Love at once and this creates an experience of bliss. We grow in that over time our bliss becomes more and more effortless. We become more skillful at creating situations we enjoy – and joy, peace and love become what feel normal to us in a wider and wider array of situations.

Unconditional Bliss

Though I am skilled in manifesting situations as I like, many times I find myself temporarily dissatisfied with the features of my life. I may spend 8 months living in a place where my sleep is disturbed every night as I wait for the situation to shift or the clarity that I need to move. I may face crises in the areas of health, relationships, finances – any aspect of life.

Living in close communion with your higher self doesn't mean you won't face the challenges of life. It means you will face them with your full ability to meet whatever may arise. It means you will be able to act from a stable ground of joy, inner peace, and mental clarity as you engage the situation.

The more you let your life be guided by your higher self, the more the turbulence will diminish over the course of time, but if you make your goal one related to controlling external conditions instead of mastering your inner reality, you will never stop checking to make sure the walls and doors are still there. There will always be an impending threat you have to guard against. Also, you will always be grasping after something because you will never seem to have enough to insure yourself against all possible futures. Let the goal be that of inner riches, such as clarity, peace and joy, and trust that the outer situation will gradually shift to reflect those same qualities without any manipulation from you.

It is probably easy for you to see how living as your higher self would make more clarity available to you. Since you would be looking at situations from a higher perspective that sees more of the hidden dynamics, including indirect influences and future consequences, of course better decisions could be made. It may be harder to imagine that simply shifting perspective within a troubling situation would lead to a joyful or serene experience of the situation. The situation might continue to be just as undesirable from your personality's point of view, but your experience of it would be different.

Several years ago I found myself sharing a tiny 1 bedroom apartment with a raging alcoholic and his wife. Neither of them worked so they basically slept all day while I was out at work, then argued, drank, watched TV, and chain smoked all night. Since I am allergic to tobacco, it was not only an emotionally toxic situation, but was physically poisoning me as well.

When I moved in I only met the wife, who did not tell me anyone else would be living there. The agreement was that she would take the living room as her bedroom and I would have the regular bedroom.

The first night I was there her estranged husband decided to return and they celebrated the event by having what to me amounted to a full blown party beginning at 2 am. As inconvenient as that was, I would have welcomed nightly revelries if it would have spared me the constant fighting that was to follow. That one night apparently represented the sum of all their affection for one another. A steady stream of yelling, insults, and slamming doors became the norm thereafter.

Since I was only working a part-time temp job I was barely making ends meet and had no money saved. It seemed I could not move. Yet it was while living in that violent, unhealthy environment that I manifested my dream job. You may recall from the first chapter how the highest paying, most rewarding job of my life miraculously came together for me at the final hour through a process of maintaining my inner peace and continuing to clarify my intentions for work. What I didn't mention in the first chapter was that I was actually maintaining that depth of peace while living in utter chaos.

Not only was I able to anchor myself in a field of inner peace during the two months I lived there, but I also found myself drifting off to sleep each night with a feeling of floating in the loving arms of the Buddha. The constant barrage of curses and insults, the smell of alcohol and cigarette smoke wafting under my bedroom door, it was all like a dream.

As my embodied higher self, I watched the dream with great alertness and responded from a place of integrity and strength. Many times I would ask them to step away from my door if they were going to carry on a conversation or go over to the window if they were going to smoke. I engaged the situation fully and advocated for myself to the point where the husband, who eventually started directing most of his anger at me, threatened to move out himself.

I am nothing like a doormat, however peaceful I may be. Within the dream of conflict there was an unshakable reality of joy, peace, and security within me and I acted from that center. I knew who I was. I was Spirit appearing in human form, and I was claiming what I needed in the situation until I could manifest something more desirable.

After two months, the perfect apartment fell into my lap and I moved into a situation as heavenly as the previous one had been hellish. By staying in my center while continuing to engage the situation, I manifested outside myself the same peace and joy my higher self had been generating within me.

What would have happened if I had engaged the situation with my personality instead of my spirit? What if I had decided that living there had to mean suffering because, gee, how could anyone not suffer under such conditions? According to the laws of manifestation, even once I left there I would have found myself in another place of suffering, one that simply had different outward features. And I probably would not have even been able to move as quickly as I did.

It is hard to move anywhere without savings, but especially in Manhattan. Thankfully, the woman who rented me my new apartment felt so good about me based on my peaceful, cheerful energy that she let me move in without a security deposit! In fact, she felt so connected with me just from talking on the phone that before she even met me she scheduled my viewing of the apartment ahead of all the other appointments she had set.

Once we met she was even more sure I was the one. She told me she was going to cancel all the other appointments as soon as I left and made me an official offer right there on the spot. I was the only one who ever saw that apartment – a sun-drenched 3 bedroom on the Upper West Side of Manhattan, two blocks from the Hudson River, fully furnished, with a rent of just $400 a month per room! I lived there most of the remainder of my time in New York and it was just as much of a blessing as it sounds like it would be.

Moving into closer communion with your higher self doesn't mean you will be spared all unpleasantness in life. In fact, you may face some utterly horrific situations. Nor does it prevent you from experiencing a great deal of stress due to those situations. Life continues to force you to grow. It still gives you one opportunity after another to define who you are and choose to grow on a path of joy instead of one of suffering, to choose understanding and forgiveness instead of blame or guilt. That means that suffering, blame, or guilt will be the obvious option, the one that doesn't require any growth.

The blessing of living life in partnership with your higher self is that you will find the means within you to rise to those challenges and actually grow in wisdom. You get to be bliss even while living in what seems like hell. You learn how to turn an image of hell into one of heaven. You don't just stay there with the idea that hell is good enough. You choose again, continuing to define your life for yourself as the conscious creator you are.

Isn't that what we are collectively doing on this planet, learning to reveal heaven within a world that seems to be built entirely around conflict? To do this, we need more and more people living as their higher selves within day to day life.

The more we see with the eyes of Spirit, which we can do through our connection to our higher selves, the more we discover that this world is very much like a dream of conflict. Spirit's reality, on the other hand, is an experience of heaven. More and more, we wish to live in Spirit's reality and see through all the murky stuff of which hellish dreams are made.

Living a life of bliss does not depend on creating enjoyment. That is just icing on the cake. Living in bliss is primarily a matter of learning how to see with the eyes of Bliss. You don't need to change the world. You need to discover a reality that is beyond all worlds. And this you will indeed do, since heaven is within your true nature, and the nature of all that exists.

Please don't make the mistake of thinking that I am saying, "God is here within you and all things." I am saying, "God isn't here, and neither are you." That is because "here" doesn't really exist. This realm of imperfection is not real. Only Divine perfection truly exists, so if you exist at all, you exist as that.

In the next chapter I will establish these ideas more fully, but for now I simply want to emphasize this: The greatest joy is that of revealing your true nature.

As we close this section of the book, I hope you go forward with an understanding of just how natural your happiness is. I hope you no longer see yourself as powerless, useless, or lacking in any way. Now you have seen the secrets of triple happiness: the joy of self-service creation, the joy of giving, and the joy of being. And you have seen one example after another of just how these joys play out in everyday life.

Pause a moment now to reflect on what it means for your life to have this clarity and focus. Ask yourself what it means to you to be bliss.

Try This For 3 Days:

It is hard to hit a target you can't see. What is the vision of your happiness like? When you think of a life of miracles, what situations, people, and things do you see in your life? When you think of being a blessing to others, what does that mean to you? What kinds of things do you do and how do others respond? What about the image of what it means to be fully embodying Spirit at all times, what does that look like?

I have often debated within myself whether in prayer I tell Spirit what I want and It manifests it for me or whether in prayer I gain glimpses of what Spirit wants for me then use my free-will to open myself to receive. I tend to think that either can be the case, depending on whether I decide to manifest conditions that satisfy my ego or ones that satisfy my spirit. If you want to grow on a path of mixed joys, manifest from your ego. If you want to grow on a path of unwavering joy, let Spirit tell you what you want.

Begin and end each of the next three days by going into a state of deep prayer or meditation then asking your higher self the above questions. Listen and reflect. Write as much as you can in your journal so that at the end of the three days you can easily compare each day's visions without having to rely upon your memory. Note which answers changed or stayed the same over the course of the three days. Try to see which parts of the vision seem to be originating out of fear based thinking and which reflect an awareness of unlimited connectedness.

Try this for three days and clarify your intentions at the highest level possible.

4 THE POWER OF CONVICTION

Entertain this possibility: Ideas are all that truly exist within this Universe.

I want this book to take you beyond inspiration. I want you to be able to use it to transform your life from one of partial satisfaction, or maybe even utter despair, into one of complete fulfillment. In order for this to happen, you must apply yourself to the exercises given with full focus of attention, positive expectation, and perseverance. And before you will make such a commitment, you must believe that your efforts are likely to pay off.

Many of you read the examples and explanations given in the first chapter and instinctively knew the approach would work for you just as it has worked for me. By now you have been applying the principles given and seeing some results, so you know from personal experience and need no convincing.

This chapter is written for the rest of you, the skeptics and hedgers, because you can't hedge at this. If you have more confidence in the idea that life can't possibly work the way I've described than you do in the possibility that it does in fact work this way, you are going to confirm the stronger belief. The principles will actually be working for you – you simply will be using them to defeat yourself instead of realizing your hopes and dreams, so it will appear to you that they don't work.

This is the problem with divided motivations. Whether the division results from an unconscious belief that you don't deserve to be happy or from fully conscious cynicism, the end result is the same. You will create according to whichever vision you hold that has the most energy feeding into it. Moreover, even if there is a slight advantage to your positive thoughts, it will take you much longer to see the desirable results materialize if you are also energizing doubt. You will be pulling yourself in opposite directions at once.

My goal is that after reading this chapter you will understand that: 1) this world is in fact more like a dream than a solid thing; 2) you can transform what may seem like a nightmare into what is clearly a happy dream; and 3) you can even wake up from the dream altogether and return to the awareness of your eternal wholeness.

I want you to understand all of this as something truly achievable, not just wishful thinking. However, since I realize many people have an easier time relating to stories, even hypothetical ones, than they do to straight scientific theory, I will begin with an "imagine this" scenario, then give you the science later.

Making It Seem Real – And Seem Really Good

Think of a table laid out with 10 little red balls lined up side-by-side at one end and a yellow string stretched across the opposite end of the table representing the finish-line.

Imagine that each red ball represented something you want to see happen in your life. The yellow finish-line is the point at which the desire has materialized. All you have to do to make anything a part of your reality is to blow on a particular ball – direct enough energy at it – to move it all the way over the table and across the finish-line.

Easy, right? There is just one complication. All of this is taking place in a dimension of reality you can't perceive. It is all just thoughts and beliefs to you until a ball actually crosses the finish-line and becomes real in this dimension.

Now imagine that you started blowing at the first red ball so that, unbeknownst to you, it moved forward a few inches. After a month or two not seeing anything happen, you decide to switch balls. You begin directing your energy at the second ball. It also inches forward, but now you are distracted. You wake up the next day having forgotten all about the second ball and totally obsessed with the third ball. So you begin to work at it.

By the end of a year you have successfully moved all ten balls half way across the table. The only problem is, since you have to get a ball all the way across the table before it materializes, it seems to you that nothing has happened. You interpret the experience as conclusive evidence that you are inept at manifesting anything you want. Maybe this is a cold, cruel world in which all hopes are denied, or maybe it's just that the Universe particularly hates you. Either way, there is one thing you know for sure. Life is hard and dreams don't come true.

Of course, the real lesson, which any higher self could tell you, is that dreams always come true, but if you're easily discouraged you'd better pick one at a time and stick to it long enough to see some results. In fact, this example makes the process seem much more difficult than it really is. You don't even have to blow on the balls to get them across the table. All you have to do is look at them!

The power of your attention is enough. Let your higher self supply the wind. All you have to do is make sure your goals don't contradict one another then focus on each one long enough for your higher self to do its work. This is enough to attract the opportunity you want. Then just add a little action to take advantage of the opportunity and you're set. Now could it be any simpler than that? This really was meant to be easy.

Not only does this work at the level of manipulating everyday reality to make happy outcomes appear within this dream life we share, but it even works when we turn our intentions towards the ultimate goal. We can use the power of attention to help us wake up from the dream altogether and return to a full experience of our naturally whole and blissful Self. We can do this because we are playing within a world of personal perceptions and private meaning making – essentially, ideas.

Thought can create experience within this world because our experience of this world is created entirely out of sensory perceptions and mental conceptions that give meaning to those perceptions. It's created out of thoughts.

Which is not to dismiss the significance of your life experience. Within this illusion, everything that happens is very real to other parts of the illusion (such as your body and emotional system). The reason we want to understand that we are experiencing an illusory reality is so that we will be more responsible about what we create, not less so. When you really get that you are the one scripting the contents of the localized experience of this grand illusion which you know as "your life story," then you will gain the freedom to create a masterpiece life.

If you want to live in bliss, it is vitally important that you truly understand that you are like an artist who has created an amazingly realistic imaginary world. What is this world of yours really like? What is actually there within what you call solid stuff and how can it be affected? I have given you a metaphor, but now I want to get down to the physics of the matter. Let us turn to an examination of some of the most advanced findings of modern science and see how they help explain the phenomena we see and our roles as creators.

An Interesting Set of Ideas

Everything that you perceive is occurring within a dimension. Recall from high school physics class that a dimension is an independent direction of possible movement. In everyday terms, if you are moving it is always right or left, backwards or forwards, up or down, or some combination of the three. There is no other possibility for how you can move within this 3-dimensional world.

That said, I ask again, consider the possibility that all that exists within this Universe are ideas. What if there was no real substance making up this world of ours, nothing beyond rules governing movement. And rules are just mutually agreed upon concepts, which can hardly be called a solid thing.

According to String Theory, as we follow the cells of our bodies into their atoms, then their quarks, and eventually their strings, we come at last to the 11 dimensions of possible movement that regulate which elementary particle will manifest. If certain microscopic strings oscillate within this cute little curly shaped dimension, we get an electron. If a different set of rules limiting movement apply, we get a muon. And so on. Dimensions determine masses and charges and thereby select what "matter" gets to appear in our reality.

Moving back up the scale, we combine all these microscopic parts and eventually get a human being, versus a rock, versus a volcano. Even within a human, emotional reactions also can be traced to habitual chemical reactions within our physical system which affect our psycho-neural system. And of course, these chemicals are all generated from the atoms, built upon the quarks, comprised of strings, which move within certain dimensions in just such a way as to create....

Again and again, we come back to the rules limiting motion as the building blocks for all that comes after. These conceptual limitations make up the world with which we are familiar. Yet rules are really just ideas. And a world built purely out of ideas is little more than an illusion. How easily can you change your mind?

Yet beyond all concepts, there is a pure awareness that is not a product of this world of illusions. It has always been whole, unchanging, full of love, and in a word, perfect. We will look at that Ultimate realm of existence more deeply later. First, let's take a closer look at the science explaining the physical composition of our world and examine the malleability of the components of our dream.

Mostly Empty Space

All matter is composed of atoms. An atom is tiny - about ten millionths of a millimeter across. To try to grasp the significance of "ten millionths of a millimeter" think of it this way, if you enlarged an apple to be the size of the entire Earth, each atom within this immense apple would still only be the size of a baseball. Imagine a planet packed with an astounding number of baseballs. Seem like a lot of stuff, but actually it's mostly a planet packed with a lot of empty space. To understand why, we must then look inside our "baseball-atoms" to see what they're made of.

In the early 1900's the British physicist Lord Rutherford bombarded atoms with alpha waves and discovered that atoms consist of vast regions of space in which very small particles called electrons orbit a nucleus, just like the Earth orbits the sun. The atom's nucleus is 100,000 times smaller than even our tiny little atom. (Think of a pinhead in the middle of a football stadium to imagine the nucleus relative to the atom.) So now we have this tiny atom with an even tinier nucleus and about 99.9999% empty space in which unimaginably tiny electrons are swirling around.

Essentially everything appearing solid to our human senses consists almost entirely of empty space. It is the amazingly small electrons whizzing around the nucleus of the atom at astounding speeds that gives atoms their solid appearance. Our measuring devices (hands, eyes, etc.) are just too large and insensitive relative to the particles they are encountering for us to accurately perceive what is there.

Another analogy that may help you imagine the composition of all matter within our physical world would be to think of a grain of salt in the middle of the dome of St. Peter's Cathedral with minute specks of dust whirling around it at speeds over 200,000 miles/hr. I think you can understand why that might be a little confusing to the untrained eye – especially once we shrink each element back down to its actual microscopic size where the "cathedral" is only a tiny fraction of a millimeter wide. It all looks and feels quite real. But is it? What is really there?

Even if we stop at this level, which was understood a hundred years ago, we still have mostly empty space making up our world. But actually the situation gets much more ephemeral. Even the tiniest constituents of the atom we have as yet considered, the electrons, are made up of still smaller parts called quarks, and theoretical physics has determined these quarks are made up of even tinier parts called strings. Remember the tiny loops vibrating within multiple dimensions to create the elementary particles? Theoretical physicists refer to those as strings. And in terms of size, forget about cathedrals; if you were to expand an atom to be the size of the entire Universe, a string would be about the size of an average tree!

What's more, no one has been able to find one of these strings experimentally. They are theorized to be there because their existence is necessary to make all our other theories make sense. Even if they are real, as mentioned earlier, it is only their patterns of multi-dimensional vibration that give rise to what we call physical matter (the elementary particles). And that vibration is governed by limitations on possible directions of movement, apparently within 11 dimensions.

In a nutshell, at the most fundamental level we can find, the physical world is a complex conceptual system presenting mutually agreed upon interpretations for what is there, but no absolute substance that could actually be called "there" without the conceptual system that describes it. All that we know about this world is what we have thought about it, not some absolute truth about what it actually may be. All measurable experience relies upon and is limited to the particulars of the equipment doing the measuring, and that equipment is always a product of the very belief structure being measured!

Moreover, matter is not only rather hard to find, but extremely impressionable. Many people are by now familiar with the fact that in sub-atomic research it has been shown that the presence of the experimenter affects the results of the experiment. For example, when particle accelerators are used to smash atoms, the electrons released can either appear as waves or particles, depending on which the experimenter is measuring at the time. Common sense would indicate that it has to be one or the other within its basic nature and therefore at all times, but experience shows that what it is depends on what you are looking for.

Experiment after experiment has revealed amazing characteristics of sub-atomic building blocks for the physical world, suggesting incredible malleability for what we call "solid" matter. The scope of this book doesn't allow me to share the research with you but I want to strongly encourage you to read Michael Talbot's *The Holographic Universe*, Lynne McTaggart's *The Field*, Dr. Masaru Emoto's *The Hidden Messages in Water*, and physicist Brian Greene's *The Elegant Universe*.

I would particularly like to urge you to read Talbot's book. It makes the strongest case I have ever encountered in establishing that we essentially project this illusory 3-D reality using our collective mind and magnetize personal experiences using the attention of our individual minds. His book then goes even further to present an impressive array of research findings explaining just how it is we do it.

Dr. Emoto's book presents incredible research he has done using high speed photography to capture images of water as it freezes. He has been able to reveal how the microscopic structure of water is affected by human thoughts towards it. His work demonstrates that harmonious, loving thoughts create healthy, harmonious patterns within the physical structure of water, while hateful and negative thoughts create disharmony and "broken off" areas that are very similar to the way cancer seems to function in the human body.

Given that you and everyone around you is composed of 45-50% water (depending on age and gender), it should not be surprising that your prayers for yourself and others can actually heal. Just remember to make it a prayer of affirmation, seeing the person healthy, being grateful for that health, and feeling loving towards the person – rather than seeing them as unhealthy, in need of health, and fervently wishing they would become well.

Between those four books there are accounts of hundreds of experiments that concur on one point: our everyday conceptions about the world in which we live are limited to say the least, and delusional to put it bluntly.

You may reasonably wonder, "If all of this has been known for so long, why is it not common knowledge in terms of how people live their lives?" Being social animals certainly does have its drawbacks. One is that we tend to like to go with the flow, fit in, agree with consensus reality.

I recall an experiment I learned of during my counseling degree program in which subjects were asked to choose the shorter of two lines. They did so both alone and then again within groups. When they were alone they consistently were able to identify the shorter line, but the group situation was rigged for the purposes of the experiment.

Each group had only one experimental subject and was otherwise filled with volunteers who were instructed by the researcher to always pick the wrong line. In that group situation, the subjects agreed with the consensus and picked the wrong line about 35% of the time. This was consistent even when one of the lines was as much as 7 inches longer. When the experiment was explained to the subjects later and they were asked why they had chosen the longer line as the shorter one when in the group, most of them insisted that they had not been trying to conform. They actually perceived the one they had picked as being the shorter line.

Even after reading all of this, you will still get up and walk out into a world in which the consensus assumes that physical matter can only be affected by physical force, that life is a struggle in which there is competition for limited resources, and that the operation of cause and effect within our lives is purely physical. The question is, what will you dare to see and how will you choose to live?

Ditto

These "modern discoveries" have been central teachings of a number of spiritual lineages for hundreds of years. Let me close the chapter by sharing a corresponding teaching from Vajrayana Buddhism with you.

Advanced Tibetan Buddhist meditation practices of Dzogchen and Mahamudra and the Buddhist concept of Ultimate Bodhicitta both rely upon an understanding that this world is an illusion. In Dzogchen meditation you begin with an understanding that all that arises in your experience is just the play of Mind. Thoughts, feelings, perceptions, and sensations come and go within your awareness without any prodding from you. It is nothing personal. It is simply the natural flow of this illusory system. With this understanding you then sit and watch your inner experience. You practice seeing the true nature of your human experience within the controlled and focused environment of your meditation room.

As you get up from the meditation cushion and move out into the world, you continue to remind yourself that all you see or otherwise experience is this same flow that is being initiated by the play of Mind. This Mind is not linked to a personal brain. It is a shared mind that makes up this shared dreamlike reality of ours. There is also a localized level of personal experience, but this private subset of Mind operates the same as the collective Mind – it is characterized by a habitual flood of perceptions, just with the primary effect on the individual.

Through Dzogchen practice, you learn to recognize all of human experience as the display of Mind's activity. Usually people just let their minds wander without even realizing it. They let the collective Mind choose for them. That wouldn't be so bad if Mind didn't have really bad habits. I won't go into it too much here, but I think you can agree with me that whatever Mind is programming this world we see must be a little twisted. I mean, come on. Can we ever get enough war?

So Dzogchen meditation seeks to help us recognize the illusory nature of our experience. One benefit of this is that we then don't have to be so hung up on the contents of our experience. Recognizing the world is an illusion makes it a lot easier to be peaceful and compassionate.

But the real value of Dzogchen practice is that it points at what is beyond the illusion, that which cannot be described directly. This is where science leaves off and philosophy begins. The greatest wisdom that humans can achieve is an understanding of the limits of our ability to know that which lies beyond the concepts of duality –

beyond the constant cycling between high and low, good and bad, near and far, past and future.

Only once we let go of our rigid belief that we know (or can ever know) the ultimate truth, can we then experience the wholeness of our True Self. Then duality ends and we are no longer bound to this illusory realm of cyclical existence.

What is real within you is untouchable, eternally whole and perfect. It is beyond the level of Mind, beyond this dream-reality entirely. It cannot be found with an electron microscope nor measured by even the most advanced theoretical physics. This brings us to the concept of Ultimate Bodhicitta.

"Bodhicitta" refers to the wish to advance spiritually so that one can better help others. Basically, the more you are, the more you have to give. Ultimate Bodhicitta goes further to combine this urge to benefit others with an understanding that those others only "exist" conceptually, and so do you. Helping happens, but there is really no helper and no helped. Helping takes place within a highly subjective, made up world in which you act to free beings from their belief in suffering, not the imaginary suffering itself.

There are many levels along the way, but the person who truly achieves Ultimate Bodhicitta has awakened from the dream completely. He is free of all the theories and beliefs of this self-referencing conceptual system. He experiences the wholeness and perfection of his original state. Whatever he then encounters in life is recognized as a reflection of that original perfection, however distorted that reflection may appear to be. All that arises is fully experienced by him as heaven in disguise, as nirvana within samsara. No longer is there any duality causing him to perceive this as desirable and that as undesirable. He dwells constantly within an experience of the Ultimate All.

Since this "Ultimate All" is beyond dualities of past and future, It cannot be described by conceptual language in such a way as to make It truly known. Eternally present, It can only be found in your direct experience of the present moment. This experience is sometimes called epiphany, revelation, or Prajna. This "Ultimate All" is sometimes called the luminous emptiness, Light, Truth, Spirit, or God. It is important to note that no matter what term is used, the terms only point around the thing and can never truly convey knowledge of It.

When the person who is fully immersed within a constant experience of union with Spirit encounters our highly impressionable world of what appears to be solid matter, his effect is to foster perfection in the people and situations he encounters. This happens spontaneously because perfection is all he can conceive with his powerfully focused mind, a mind that is connected to the creative power of that which is beyond the limits of illusory Universes. He creates with the full power, clarity and harmony of the Truth behind him. He is therefore a spontaneous healer and peacemaker.

The achievement of Ultimate Bodhicitta is the most useful long-range goal. We want to make pretty dreams in the short run, but ultimately the only thing that will permanently get us out of the cycle of hopes, joys, fear of loss, suffering, hope, and so on, is to wake up from the dream itself. Whatever else we pursue in life, we should always be putting at least some of our energy towards the goal of waking up, and personally I prefer to put that goal first.

The more we open to an awareness of the eternal perfection beyond the illusory world of conditions – with all its hopes, satisfactions, disappointments, shame, blame, and fear – the more freedom we gain. We can free ourselves from the shackles that make up our comfortably familiar imprisonment simply by being willing to open our minds. Freedom is a measure of the ability to release our conceptual beliefs about the rules of our existence and gain an experience of the unlimited reality beyond all ideas.

However long it may take, this opening and relaxing is inevitable for us all. Within all things there is a natural drive towards freedom. Heisenberg's Uncertainty Principle establishes this, and so does the behavior of every cornered animal. The more you confine a thing, the wilder it gets. Scientifically, the more narrowly you establish where a particle is located, the less you can predict its velocity, and vice versa. Nature does not allow itself to be pinned down.

Similarly, the more freedom you allow, the more peaceful the situation gets. By freedom I don't mean the right to act irresponsibly, for there is always a consequence to any decision. For now we hope to gain the freedom to create. Ultimately it is freedom of being we aspire to. We will all someday be completely free, existing in complete union with that which does not swear an allegiance to any theory of man.

This is not a question of speculation. The rules that eventually create a system of atoms, cells, and bodies are operating within numerous dimensions to create this illusion right now. And eternity is resting within itself beyond that cosmic dance, completely unlimited within this very moment. There are however questions that are worth asking. Will you be a conscious creator or a puppet for the amusement of Mind? Do you dare to move beyond the realm of creation entirely and rest within your true being? Which do you choose right now?

There are three kinds of faith. Faith of belief is the most shallow. It comes from accepting what one has been told without analysis or personal experience. Faith of reason is more substantial. It results from inference. We spot the pattern within what is known for sure and use it to fill in the gaps, thereby developing an intuitive sense of what is true. It is this faith that I have sought to help you develop within this chapter. But the most dependable form of faith is the faith of experience, and for that you must thoroughly test the theories in your own life and see what happens. I hope you will. Namaste.

Try This For Three Days:

Start the next three days with a brief reflection on the main understanding of this chapter. First begin by setting your intention: "I want to see beyond the veils of this illusory reality. I choose to see beyond. I will see beyond."

Then begin to examine the solidity of your body. What exactly is your body made of at the most fundamental level you can find? Is your body your blood? Is it your skeleton? Is it the atoms themselves? What exactly is it that makes a body a body?

Reflect upon the abundance of space within the atoms that make up your body. Think of that grain of salt at the center of St. Peter's Cathedral with specks of dust whirling around it. Imagine that your body was that cathedral and that your atoms were that swirl of salt and dust within an expanse of empty space. Can you go even further to find the still smaller strings that make up the salt and dust? What about the oscillations of the strings within numerous dimensions?

Follow the hierarchical architecture of concepts down to its smallest level, until you find the solid stuff that constitutes your body. If you are able to find anything, you've got the entire world of experimental physicists beat, because they can't.

For three days spend some time sitting in full awareness of all the space within you. Pay attention to what is there, or not there, within you as deeply as you can. Inquire. Explore. Release.

5 THE POWER OF SELF-KNOWLEDGE

In traditional magic it is said that to know a thing's name is to have power over it. While I don't care much for magic, I do recognize the wisdom of that understanding. Knowledge is power.

What is your true name? I don't mean a proper name like Sue or Joe. I mean, if you looked closely at the deepest layers of how you respond to your inner and outer world, what would you see? How do you shape personal meaning out of the hazy, ambiguous mirage of our collective lives? What is your belief about what life in this world is really like for humans? What is going on in your experience right now? What sensations are you aware of? What thoughts are you thinking, and why?

Who are you in this moment? Will it be the same set of answers when you wake up tomorrow morning? How about 5 minutes from now?

According to Buddhism, if you examine yourself thoroughly you will discover that you are a constantly fluctuating composite of the following parts (please study this chart thoroughly, as an understanding of it is assumed throughout the rest of this book):

Parts of Self	Characteristics
Form	Physical Matter
Perception	Input received through the sense organs (eyes, ears, etc.)
Conception	Thought, making meaning out of sensory input
Volition	Habit - Momentum/inertia, the impulse that triggers what arises within the other parts of the self; karmic conditioning
Consciousness	The Witness point of view

Based on this chart we can see that habit/volition controls what arises within the parts of physicality/form, sensation/perception, and thought/conception. The witness/consciousness watches. It is the perspective that sees the whole instead of the parts, looking at the situation from the broadest point of view. It sees all of time as now and all of place as here. Consciousness is still a part of your individuality (your incarnation within the illusion of duality), but it was the first doorway you came through when you appeared to split away from the wholeness of Spirit, and it is the final doorway you will take as you appear to find your way back.

Emotion is not a separate part of the individual self, but it is a fluctuating inner process worth noting. Emotions are what we perceive as inner sensation when thoughts trigger the release of certain neuro-chemicals. Within manifestation work, emotion is an empowering medium that enhances the creative effect of thoughts. Within the development of wisdom, emotion is a communication medium, conveying guidance from the spiritual self through positive and negative reactions. Since emotion is often a direct result of thought, like thought it is frequently a habitual response. In relating to the emotional medium between the parts of the self, as well as all the separate parts themselves, it is important that we draw upon the wisdom of witness consciousness.

When we witness our inner dynamics we gain the ability to choose whether we relate to physical form, sensory perception, thought and corresponding emotions, habitually or with the wisdom of our higher selves. Fresh creative responses are only possible when we move beyond habitual reactions to life.

The higher self acts with spontaneity and enlightened appropriateness at all times, never needing to react from the past or plot for the future. The higher self uses our consciousness to relate to thought, physicality, perception and emotion like a master using valuable tools.

It has no delusion that one's thoughts represent one's identity, any more than one's body does. Its self-awareness does not get lost within any of the parts of the self. It is never fooled into thinking that it is this part, that part, or nothing more than the sum of its parts. It knows its oneness with all things everywhere and realizes that what it is experiencing through your particular system of thought, emotion and physicality is just one of many possible points of view. Instead of personal isolation, self-alienation, and all the natural responses to a belief in independence which characterize "normal" life within our society, living from the perspective of the witness fosters a sense of wholeness and security within interconnectedness.

The Face of Self-Alienation

Acquainting yourself with the inner dynamics of what thoughts and emotional reactions are habitually arising within you is the first step in the development of self-knowledge. If you are to truly know yourself, you must spend some time looking inward with courage, honesty and compassion. To best understand the value of such self-knowledge, let us look at its alternative – self-alienation.

If a man believes that he is a separate, threatened being amidst many separate beings within a competitive world, he will naturally feel compelled to stand out as one of the more competent and capable beings within that world. There is an illusion of safety provided by the illusion of importance which arises in response to an illusion of separation. So what happens to this self-made man who is so important?

He is separate. He is above, he is below, wherever he is, he is not connected to the whole. He is lonely, insecure, and compulsively looking outside himself for confirmation. All his happiness depends upon an outside eye to compare him to others. Without that eye the fruits of his life do not exist.

He lives at a great distance from himself, since to look too closely into the face reflected by the mirror of direct perception is to find a reflection more honest than he can bear. Yet if only he could bear it a short while he would find that looking more deeply he discovers an even more essential truth. He would find the true security, confidence, and power of being a part of a unity that knows only self-love. But he does not look, so he does not see.

He is the one fully invested in keeping you and all others fully immersed in the game of self-importance.

Without you, his audience and competition, how can he define himself or establish his worth? If you walk off the field, who will he play with?

He is a sad man who is suffering greatly behind his armor of independence and aggression. If you know him, please say a prayer for him. Send him love and understanding. Forgive him the destructiveness inflicted upon himself and others due to his condition, but do not indulge him. Do not compete with him. Do not envy him. And do not let him pull you into his nightmare.

It is true that this life is like a dream, but I want you to make it a happy dream. I want you to be able to view your life with full consciousness and sincerely say, "I like the way I dream." So do not let yourself be seduced into the pursuit of illusory fulfillment by those who have never known any peace. Work hard at developing an honest understanding of who you are so that you may discover the connectedness and love of that truth, instead of deepening your sense of isolation and vulnerability by building up a defense of emotional detachment and self-alienation.

Along the way to full self-understanding you still have to act. If you want to escape the egoist's fate, do the opposite of what he does. Instead of seeking to make yourself more important than those around you, choose to acknowledge and rejoice in the gifts and talents of others. Even if they perceive it incorrectly and think you are admitting their superiority, do not let that stop you. So long as your heart is truly free of envy it isn't your responsibility what they misunderstand. Just stay in your truth and anticipate that sooner or later the truth will be made known without your forcing it center stage.

It is easy to take joy in the talents and accomplishments of others when you remember that they are you. There is, after all, only one of us. They are a different reflection of the all-pervading light, but they do not absorb all the light any more than the moon steals the sun from you. There is plenty to go around.

Instead of competing with others, celebrate them and you will have surrendered your belief in separation and replaced it with a belief in connectedness. You will then be able to join with the flow of healing, love, and peace in this world and know it as yourself, for this is how your higher self views the world. As your embodied higher self, your true self, this beauty and grace will fill your life, manifesting its nature in every corner of your life with each out breath.

So where the man of separation chooses to hate this and lust after that, you will do differently. Remembering that there is only one of us, you will instead embrace diversity and use discrimination to know what you truly need and what is just greed. Why would you want to horde everything for yourself at the expense of others who need it right now? Would your foot store blood for future use and let your hand fall off for lack of it now? Of course not.

And why would you anger at anyone? If you realize that separation by its very nature is an illusion, a dream, why would you choose to end your joy and sense of inner lightness and expansiveness by embracing the contraction of anger or resistance? Isn't it draining to live life with a defensive stance? Is it possible to let it go? Can you respond effectively without anger?

The perceived offender is really just an aspect of yourself causing offense. Be gentle and forgiving towards yourself. Do not anger so easily at your imperfection. We are in the process of waking up to our inner Divinity and we make many mistakes out of ignorance, but we are innocent like little children. We are a reflection of the One Light and so We are a reflection too of one another. Forgive yourself your imperfection and you will find that patience and acceptance come easily to you in dealing with others, so long as you continue to remember that they are in fact different aspects of you.

Do not be like the desperate man of separation. Do not be hard, demanding and lonely. Instead throw wide your doors. Open your heart and embrace all of life as an equal, indeed, as your self. Replace the habits of your separate self with those of your universal self so that you may enjoy the beauty and grace of life as a Divine being at play in the fields of the Lord.

Release the habit of pride and find a loving community of equals that rejoices in your gifts and talents. Trade the habit of envy for enthusiasm and zest for life as you act to benefit others. Let go of your habitual aggression and find a world in which you are safe – free to explore and express in innocence. Trade greed for a world of justice and peace, grasping for fulfillment, and lack for abundance.

Then transcend the limitations of defining a separate self completely, so that all that is false within you may disappear and that which is untouchably true may stand naked in your sight. It is this last freedom we will look at in the next chapter on innocence.

Before addressing the power of innocence, I want to share with you an example of how I came to identify the inner dynamic that was holding me back the most so that I could focus on releasing it. This sort of delving for self-understanding is a key component of the path to freedom, since it would take a lifetime to peel away every layer of our conditioning one at a time. We must find the most rigid patterns locking us into false self-identities and actively engage those patterns in a way that allows for freedom.

Following the Breath Inward

A few months ago I traded healing sessions with a friend. We started our trade with him doing a session for me. He explained that he would be there as a reflection of me, but that I was to stay focused within my own internal process, watching my breath and whatever thoughts or emotions arose. We sat in this manner for about two hours, me reporting on my inner experience and him skillfully asking questions to support the process.

First I became aware that I was holding my breath and had to intend to breathe freely rather than letting it happen naturally. As I brought air fully into my body, I noticed a general feeling of anxiety whose source I couldn't identify. Over the course of the two hours this murky sense of unease revealed sadness, anger and profound patterns of disease within my family of origin, going all the way back to my great-grandmother.

These patterns were locking me into my identity as a mental being and preventing me from having the freedom to respond to life as Spirit using a mental tool. Beyond that, they were the source of a highly destructive habit I had of rejecting at least part of my experience throughout almost every moment of my life. This habitual stance of rejection was preventing me from ever fully relaxing into a sense of safety or wholeness.

As the session progressed, I realized how great a role survival had played in the life of my family. My grandmother had been the only one of 5 children to survive to the age of four. The only reason my grandmother survived was that a relative took her out of the empty house my great-grandmother had left her in alone and raised her as her own. The other children all died of neglect.

Coming out of this experience, my grandmother had a keen sense of the importance of attending to the physical needs of children. There has never been a child anywhere near her who did not have food to eat, clean clothes to wear, and the confidence of knowing there would be a roof over their heads in the depths of winter. She has made a lifelong commitment to giving others what someone once gave her when she needed it most – physical security.

As often happens, the focus on the provision of one need completely eclipsed the importance of others. While she was keenly aware of the physical needs of children, including a good education so that they would be able to support themselves in later life, she had no understanding of the value of emotional security. It was in this area that the pattern of neglect survived into another generation in my family.

The matter was made even worse by the fact that she let her own neglectful mother take care of her grandchildren! My grandmother had reconciled with her mother in her youth and fully supported her from that time until my great-grandmother's death at the age of 81. That is who babysat me from birth to age 6.

During the session I realized for the first time why I always treated baby dolls with such careless disregard. When I was a child I never wanted baby dolls. If someone gave one to me I would toss it under the bed or the bureau and forget all about it. I always thought it was because I knew even then that I never wanted to be a mother, but in the session it hit me that my treatment of the dolls probably reflected how I felt treated myself. I can guess that my great-grandmother likely showed the same disinterest in caring for me she had shown with her own children who died from neglect. I was lucky I was only left with her during the work day and had a large number of caregivers every evening.

Still, I came away from the experience feeling like: A) I was not wanted in this world; B) My pure being was not enough for me to have value; and C) I was not safely cared for. Hunger cries would not necessarily be answered. This was a cold, cruel world and I was helpless in it.

The survival habit pattern I developed to deal with this existential insecurity was that of being smart and obedient, never expressing negative emotions and always impressing everyone with perfect grades. My family valued education very highly and I was the star in that regard. We were poor in all that related to the enjoyment of life, such as toys or birthday celebrations, but rich in anything that promised improved chances for survival – albeit according to a very limited conception of what children need to survive.

Out of this family system I have seen a great deal of disease and despair. Suffice to say that it has been a painful teaching for us all. What I came to understand in the "delving" session with my friend was that the survival habit of tight self-regulation (to the point of emotional suffocation) led to suppressed rage and a secondary habit of rebellion. The habit I most needed to transcend was that of constantly rebelling against all of existence out of anger at having been so deprived as a child. I felt deeply wronged by a world that apparently awarded children who I knew were no more kind, gentle or loving than me with extraordinary abundance and what appeared to be the warmest embrace, while leaving me on the outside of every fence.

That anger was the fuel for my suicide attempts, as well as my destructive behavior, throughout my childhood. And the sadness that came with it was the source of my depression and withdrawal from life. The anxiety was the product of the precarious position of having to constantly prove my worth in order to feel I would get the care I needed from the human family.

As a child, and well into adulthood, I truly felt that this was a cruel, dangerous world in which I had no inherent value and in which I was only given provisional safety as long as I could prove some worth by displaying intelligence. And I certainly had better not be an inconvenience to anyone. I hated that world and I hated myself. I wanted out, out of life in general, and out of the present moment in particular.

Just as extremely as I had practiced placation in early childhood, in my teens I embraced resistance as my habitual response to life. Instead of having no boundaries and compulsively saying, "yes" to anything anyone asked of me, my new habit became that of saying, "No," to everything. "No, I won't believe what you are telling me. No, I won't arrive on time. No, I won't smile. No, I won't breathe in or breathe out any more than is absolutely necessary. No, no, no, no, no!"

I refused to fully embrace the contents of any moment. My mind was always focused on my rejection of some part of whatever was in my experience. Through this rejection of experience, I was acting out my rejection of the world of humans which I refused to forgive for being so astoundingly imperfect. I was saying no to human life itself.

This is the mantra of disease. This is the mantra of my family, and maybe yours too. It is a habit that must be broken. The path to freedom lies through understanding, forgiveness, and a commitment to creating new, healthy habits of response. In place of the habit of saying no to life there must grow a habit of saying yes. Yes. Yes, yes, yes, yes, yes, yes, yes! I accept this moment, just as it is right here and now without any hedging or conditionals. Yes, I choose life.

More than that, I choose to recognize my identity as a being that was never damaged by any of what arose in my experience. I have always been whole, safe, and in complete abundance. I am Spirit. I came into this life knowing what awaited me, fully prepared, and in full acceptance of my role. I structured this experience so that I could learn the pain of the world. I see in its cruel treatment of me its own self-hatred and I came wishing to help heal that wound and bring a message of forgiveness.

Truly, there is nothing for me to forgive, since I was never touched by any of it, but the wounded self-concept bound to this personality must be willing to forgive before it will stop its war against the present moment and allow me to emerge. It must be willing to release its resistance to the full experience of life since that is an inescapable aspect of oneness with me, the Unity.

As the unlimited Self there is nothing to forgive, but as the illusory self-identity that is bound to this one dream-like lifetime I offer this so that freedom may become possible: I forgive everyone who has ever disregarded my cries for help. I forgive those who returned my affections with callous disregard or met my insecurities with ridicule. I forgive those who denied my value and taught me to do the same. I forgive every person who ever stole from me, lied to me, or attacked me in any way. I forgive those who walked away when I needed them most and those who hated me for reminding them of their own vulnerability. I forgive this world, just as I forgive myself for every hurtful word I ever spoke. I forgive you, and I am ready to see you be completely happy.

I can forgive because I understand. Through the wisdom of my higher self, who was there through it all, I can see that every act of violence I directed outward reflected the violence I felt against myself. Similarly, I see that others' disregard of my needs and feelings was just a reflection of callousness they had experienced themselves and the hatred they carried towards their own vulnerability. I see the pain of the world in the pain it inflicted upon me and I see its drive for self-obliteration in the mechanisms of its society.

My life is a call to you. Please forgive. Make peace with life. Love this world. Love your life. Love yourself. Please say yes to life. Let us not commit mass suicide. Each of us, one by one, let us learn to love ourselves and forgive all wrongs we seem to have done to others or experienced at their hands. It was all a dream of viciousness, turned either inward against the illusory self or outward against the illusory other, within this imaginary world of duality. We have always remained whole and untouched.

Let us practice saying yes to life. Over and over, let us greet each new moment with a willingness to be fully present and see all of what is there to be seen without denial, aggression, guilt or blame. Breathing in and breathing out – with an open, loving presence – this is the most positive act of creation there is.

Only with the most intimate and honest self-knowledge can self-acceptance be anything more than an attractive idea. Know yourself. Forgive yourself. Embrace yourself. Free yourself. It's up to you.

Try This For Three Days:

Pick a time you can be alone for at least 15 minutes without any distractions. If you don't have 15 minutes that you can do this each day, that is the most important insight about your life that you need to look at more closely.

Begin with a prayer to your higher self, the "Ultimate All," the primordial Buddha, God, or whatever metaphor resonates for you. Ask that you have the courage to see with honesty and instantly forgive whatever seeming imperfection you may encounter within yourself.

Watch your breath. Become aware of any feelings or thoughts that arise. Don't try to interpret or control what arises; just watch and keep breathing.

After a few minutes, begin to think about an area of concern in your life. Perhaps you are experiencing conflict in a relationship at home or at work. Or maybe there are financial issues causing some tension or concern.

As you begin to think about the issue, watch what happens to your breath. Note any changes. Return to looking at the feelings and thoughts arising within you now that you have touched this troubling issue. You may notice a change in the character of what arises.

Continue to watch without judging, interfering or analyzing. Understanding will emerge naturally if you look long enough without interrupting the experience or getting distracted. You will likely encounter flashes of insight. Insight pops up within an open mind. Analysis you have to work at by manipulating and controlling your mind. Allow insight and don't get lost in analysis.

Sit peacefully with whatever insights emerge, instantly forgiving any "negativity" or limitation that may reveal itself by recognizing its illusory nature as a mere idea of imperfection. The idea of imperfection is a judgment coming from a belief in duality. Release all judgments as you continue to open your mind and greet whatever is there. Continue to breathe as you observe the flowing currents of thought and feeling.

You are form (breath moving through a body), perception (sensation), and conception (thought and emotion) habitually arising in response to inner and outer stimulation, but you are also the consciousness that is watching it all. Lovingly sit with all of who you are long enough and you will eventually come to an experience of being the blissful awareness beneath all the comings and goings. You will then know yourself both in your illusory, fragmented patterning and in your essential, eternally whole truth. The choice is then yours: which will you follow?

Try it for three days, and see what you discover

6 THE POWER OF INNOCENCE

Whenever I anthropomorphize God, which I generally try not to do, I imagine this huge body sitting with one toe shoved into this tiny little shoe, tugging and pulling at it and saying, "How do we fit into these bodies?" The answer of course is, grow the shoe. Expand.

In order to expand, you must first relax the leather. It must be soft and pliable or expansion will tear it apart. So if you want to be one with the highest aspects of yourself, to embody divinity as fully as you are able to do with this life of yours, soften your idea of who you are. Open, relax, expand and embrace your present experience right here and now, just as it is. Surrender your belief in a well-defined, separate self and allow a little space to emerge. In this space your higher self may shine through all the experiences of your life.

While you conceive of yourself as a separate being who is trying to create a prosperous life, you may need to train yourself to replace thoughts about lack with thoughts of gratitude for abundance, but as your full-strength, unity-conscious higher self you don't train for anything. You just know you are one with everything - a naturally abundant state.

That is what I meant earlier when I said that in time the development of the third key to happiness would take care of the first two. When you take the point of view (POV) of your higher self, new responses are possible because you are new in every moment yourself. You aren't a thing. You're a process. As your higher self, you can be the process of creating a lesson on joyful living within the human realm.

Once you free yourself from self-identification within any (and all) of the parts of the separate self (thought, feeling, form, habit, or even individual consciousness), you gain the unlimited possibilities of Spirit. No matter how we aggrandize our achievements, the separate self-concept's point of view (POV) is always limited and inherently vulnerable. Suffering is inevitable whenever we hold the view that who we truly are is any of these separate parts.

There is no hope for stable peace of mind if we are continually getting sucked back into the point of view (POV) of the body, which sees a vulnerable, mortal self that must constantly be guarded, defended, and promoted. The physical body's POV is prone to belief in scarcity, lack and all sorts of suffering.

The POV of the emotional body is just as debilitating. It is prone to negative emotions because it is so closely linked to the doomed physical body. There is anger in defending the self against threat, sadness at the inevitability of loss, inadequacy, fear, and on and on – all arising from getting lost within a separated POV.

The POV that is lost in thoughts is probably the most damaging for Westerners. We think that we actually are our thoughts! We live from the inside of the thoughts rather than the outside. To be able to stand outside your thoughts and watch yourself thinking, simply perceiving, "Here is this thought, now here comes this one, oh there it goes and another comes now," is to be free of the tyranny of the mind.

All of us find great relief in temporary vacations from the mental POV. We usually find it by getting lost in a POV of one of the other parts. We take a hot bath and for just a moment the mind disappears into the body's experience completely. We get lost in running and experience runner's high. We get lost in sex and all that exists is the present moment and the intense pleasure within the body. And so on. Getting lost in emotions isn't usually so pleasant since it generally takes powerful negative emotions to overcome the iron grip of the mind, but sometimes we are overcome by the feeling of falling in love or our gratitude at something wonderful and unexpected someone has just done for us.

The importance of these "vacations" is not so much that they give us a much needed rest, as that they provide an open door to the POV of bliss consciousness. That is what we are after. That is where we wish to stabilize so that we will always have the ability to choose how we respond in the present, letting go of the conditioning of the past and through innocence finally getting to live as our unlimited selves.

By going through the door of sexual ecstasy without getting lost within the physical body's POV and becoming mere animals engaged in an intensely pleasurable reproductive act, we have the potential to lose ourselves entirely within the other and thereby touch the infinite. It is right there, just at our fingertips, if only we bother to reach for it. If only we are willing to expand, relax, release the bounds of where we stop and the "other" begins so that there is only the unity who is witnessing the act of love making.

By going through the door of sport there is the same chance. We can be the body pulling the tiller, the boat, the sail, the wind, and the sea all at once, instead of being a sailor. We can be the road, the shoe falling on it, the breath moving in and out, and the muscles repetitively contracting, instead of being a runner.

Whatever set of doors you choose, go through them and do it often. The goal is to use the escape paths frequently enough to make freedom an unconscious habit. Over and over, choose to direct your attention to the higher self's limitless POV so that you build a habit of responding from innocence.

Innocence and Self-identification

The idea each of us holds about who we are is one of the most difficult things to surrender. Each of us wants to be someone in particular. Every child gradually learns to move away from direct contact with the world. They go from relating as a wide open sky meeting a great, unknown expanse to relating as a fragile being that must hide behind a cloud of identity.

Society encourages the development of this facade because it wants to be able to easily sum each of us up at a glance and decide whether we are important to its aims. With many people, if you can help them get ahead or at least reflect favorably upon them by association, then you are worth knowing. If not, you will swiftly be dismissed and ignored.

Do you ever catch yourself relating to people with such efficient pragmatism? Where do you think you learned to relate to others this way? Likely it is because this is how others have related to you, thus programming another part of the machine to keep the machine running.

Which role did you decide to take? Or was a role forced on you without much input on your part? Are you the smart one? Are you the flunky? Are you the misunderstood artist? The isolated nerd? The super-achiever? The bubbly breath of fresh air? What shape is your cloud? How dense is it? Does it completely block all light or are there moments when your true being shines through?

Perhaps there are times when you are alone that you momentarily forget who you are supposed to be. Maybe when you are traveling alone and there is nothing familiar around you nor anyone to relate to you in habitual ways there is some clarity that emerges. Though even in that situation everyone you meet is trying to sum you up, they are unlikely to hit upon the unique configuration that you accept as your identity. In that incongruity there is an opening created. If you can see all misunderstandings about who you are as opportunities for escape, you are half way over the barricades already.

The innocent life is a life beyond clouds. It is a life lived free, not necessarily from the point of view of the world, but in how you relate to yourself. The innocent life is not an echo of past thoughts, words, or actions. It is a continual stream of present moment responses coming from the higher self, which is always present-centered and never habitual.

When I moved to Bali I irritated so many of my new friends because I refused to tell them what I had done for work before moving there. I was pretty tight with all information actually, because I didn't move there so that I could live as an echo of my history. I moved there to embrace a new way of being and for that the most important new ingredient was not the place, but me.

Of course, they couldn't accept not knowing so they began to speculate. Some thought my life before must have been something terrible and that was why I wanted to forget it. Others thought I must be ashamed of my past and so wanting to hide it. Still others thought I was just being dramatic and wanting to enjoy the attention of repeated interrogations about my past. Ha!

I put up with it all because I know that having people misunderstand you when they know they are making flimsy guesses is a lot better than having them misunderstand you when they think they actually know who you are. I knew that if I told them I had been a counselor in America I would have risen in esteem in many of their eyes, particularly among the Balinese, but I wasn't after strokes for my ego. I was after freedom for my being, and I found it within relative insignificance.

I am not recommending you move far away from everyone you know so that you can recreate yourself with a blank slate. You could, but unless you did so with clarity and resolve you would be likely to soon recreate the same conditions you left at home. Instead, I wish to point you towards a way of opening yourself to continual self-revelation that happens right where you are now, wherever that happens to be.

There are two primary approaches to doing this. Immersing yourself fully within the flow of all existence without resistance or detachment is the solo practitioner's method. It is available to anyone who has sufficient self-discipline to consistently attempt it and sufficient emotional maturity and courage to really do it. The second method involves relationship with helpers.

The opportunity for this new kind of relationship is not easily gained. You have to be ripe for it. Your soul has to cry out for it. You have to be so thoroughly disillusioned with worldly life, the life of a cloud within a fierce storm, that you are ready for self-obliteration if that's what it takes to be free. When that time comes you will make the call, and if you are both fortunate and alert you will see that your call is answered.

Training by the Guru

I am not a follower of gurus. Many of the people I see being called "enlightened" seem to me to simply have gained the ability to see through the veils of this illusory world with some degree of consistency. For them, this clear view is not theory or belief, but lived experience. They are able to therefore manipulate the contents of this dream with great power and skill. They are essentially master illusionists. To a noteworthy degree they have awakened to the light of Unity Consciousness and will hopefully progressively expand to embody it more and more fully.

That is all it means. It does not mean they don't have personalities, particularly in the early stages of their self-expansion. It does not mean they don't have egos. It does not mean they will never use the powers granted by their wisdom to manipulate those around them into serving their selfish aims. People aren't necessarily selfless just because they recognize their connection with others, even when that recognition is of a spiritual oneness.

That is not so hard to understand if you consider how people treat their own children. Often parents view their children as extensions of themselves, but that doesn't stop them from beating, neglecting and emotionally torturing them. Not all parents of course, but that it happens at all goes to show you the compatibility between the ideas of "universal self" and "what I can get for this part of me at the expense of that part of me."

This disclaimer given, I will tell you that I have greatly benefited from the assistance of spiritual teachers who have progressed beyond the levels of selfishness I am referring to above. One teacher in particular, who would never describe himself as enlightened, helped me a great deal.

In a true guru-disciple relationship the teacher helps the student regain his or her true nature as a clear sky by stimulating and guiding the process of the student's identity dissolution. My first Buddhist teacher was Lama Pema Wangdak. Let me share with you one example of how he helped me peel away part of one layer of my identity – that of being "the smart one."

Who Is There To Be Smart?

As I stood outside the Dharma Center waiting for Lama Pema to arrive with the distinguished guest teachers visiting from Canada, my thoughts jumped ahead in anticipation of the many ways I would please my beloved Lama. I would impress him with how competent and compliant I was. He would see that there was a great deal of benefit I could provide to the center and begin to more fully utilize my abilities.

For over a year I had been wanting to find a way into the inner circle of students privileged to help with the set up of important events and it was finally happening. There was to be an advanced teaching given by a world-renowned female lama and I was one of only 3 students there to set up in advance. I was eager and excited.

After a long wait, the car pulled up and Lama Pema stepped out. He opened the door for Jetsun Kushok, one of the most esteemed female lamas in the world and the sister of the head of the Sakya lineage of Tibetan Buddhism, and both she and another lama stepped out. The second lama turned out to be a Rinpoche, a term of respect for an accomplished teacher, and also Jetsun's husband.

I put my hands together in prayer position before my heart and bent forward in respect as the ensemble came up the stairs. As he passed, Lama Pema leaned towards me and said, "Don't run away."

Don't run away? Why would he say such a thing? Why on Earth would I ever run away? I had been begging him to accept me as his student since the first night I met him, over a year earlier. I had made my involvement with his spiritual center and his teachings the center of everything happening in my life. If there was one thing I was sure of it was that I was a dedicated student, and dedicated students don't run away.

Upstairs, the lamas went in the office and we students made tea and set up the meeting space. After a few minutes Lama Pema called me into the office. He motioned for me to sit at a small table with him and told me that he had an important errand he wanted to send me on. I eagerly acquiesced. Then he began to explain what he wanted. And explain it. And explain it.

It was a simple enough request. Basically he wanted me to make enlarged copies of the text Jetsun would be teaching from that night. Her eyesight wasn't strong enough to see the small print of the original text. If he had explained it to me that way the whole affair would have gone much more smoothly. Instead his explanation was more like this:

"If they have the 11x17 inch paper, make 3 copies per sheet. But if the only paper is 11x14, make 2 copies per sheet and turn the book lengthwise. Do you understand? Maybe I had better explain it a different way?" On and on and on, for over half an hour he explained to me how to use a photocopying machine.

As I had worked in various administrative positions on and off over 15 years, running an entire office by myself in some cases, I was not exactly seeing myself as someone who needed to be told how to run a copy machine as if I had never seen one before. What was particularly disturbing to me was that the visiting lamas were in the room with us watching us intently and fully focused on every word.

"They must think I am an idiot," I thought. "They don't know how smart I am because they have never met me before. The way he is treating me must be giving them the impression that he knows I need detailed instruction just to complete a simple task."

So I resisted. I tried to argue over him, "Yes, yes, Lama Pema. I know you want me to ..." And he would interrupt. "It sounds like you don't understand. Let me start again."

Half an hour! I tried every tactic I could think of to get him to stop and just let me go ahead and make the copies. I agreed with him. Then he asked me to explain to him what he had said. No explanation was ever good enough. So I argued with him. Shouldn't I do it this way instead? That only made him get more insistent and seem annoyed with me. Nothing I tried was working. I began to sweat profusely and my mind was overcome by inner turmoil. It felt like he had put all my emotions in a vise and was slowly tightening it.

I don't recall what finally ended our stand off, but after about 45 minutes of instruction and in a complete mental and emotional haze, I was sent to make the photocopies. Of course, no one could tell me where to go to get the copies made. I was pointed in a general direction and told that it wasn't far. So I began walking in that direction, glad to get out of that room and be on my own in the fresh air.

Thus I began to walk towards the vaguely North-west Kinko's. And I walked. And I walked. Now I was sweating because I was walking over a mile in the hot sun of a New York summer carrying a book that weighed at least 10 pounds. When I finally made it to the Kinko's, right outside the door I found a subway station for the same train that ran only one block from the Dharma center I began at. I could have used my metro card for a free ride just two stops on the train if only I had been given the one set of instructions I actually needed.

Despite my annoyance at my needless exercise for the day, I was glad to finally be at the end of my assignment. I would hand the book to the clerk, pay him whatever he wanted to make the copies for me, then take the subway back to the center.

As fate would have it, the clerk refused to make the copies for me. He informed me that there was a library stamp at the front of the book and that they were forbidden to photocopy copyrighted material, but that I could use the machines to do it myself if I wanted. I tried to get him to understand that it was the property of my library and that that was who sent me to make copies of their own book, but looking at the Tibetan text and looking at me, he was unconvinced.

Of course, it was no simple copying job. The book was so large and the pages so poorly bound that it was a challenge just keeping the entire book in position for straight copies to be produced. I kept getting pages with a character missing at one corner or another. And there were so many pages he wanted. Page 41-46, 118-191, 12a-14b, and so on. A line of impatient customers began to form behind me. Exasperated sighs grew louder and more frequent as once more I began to sweat.

I don't know how long it took, but I finally managed to make all the copies. As I came out of the Kinko's and approached the subway station outside its doors, the thought occurred to me that I could get on that same train to ride home. I didn't have to go back to the center at all. I was still offended by my treatment by Lama Pema, worn out by my entire ordeal trying to help him, and in no mood for any teachings, however important they were supposed to be.

That is when I remembered his greeting words that evening. "Don't run away." Damn him. He actually knew he intended to push my buttons before he even asked me to do him a favor and make the copies. He was playing games with me and I was not about to be bested. I just had to figure out which choice would most clearly establish that I was in control.

I used my cell phone to call my friend Kaz, a more advanced dharma student, and explained the situation to her. That was when I first learned of the guru-disciple relationship and the process of ego dissolution. She assured me that what was happening was a blessing and urged me to go back to the center to complete my first lesson successfully. I decided to follow her advice. I had already made the copies at that point and there would be many students coming from great distances to receive the teaching that depended upon my returning the text. As pissed off as I was, I wasn't able to be that childish and selfish.

By the time I got back to the center the lamas had all left for dinner and only the other students were there. "Lama Pema thought you weren't coming back," one of them said.

"Of course I came back," was my response. "Why wouldn't I?" No point giving them the impression I had considered being a very bad student when I had in fact completed my assignment as requested.

"But you took so long. Where did you go?"

I decided to dispense with politeness and just ignore that question. I went in the office and lay down on the couch until the lamas returned and the formal teaching for the evening began.

I actually felt pretty good when they first spotted me upon their return and I saw how disturbed Lama Pema looked. He had obviously been worrying about what they would do for the teaching that evening given that he was certain I would not return with the text. Served him right. Still, I couldn't help but to feel proud of myself when I saw Jetsun smile at me. I had at least pleased someone that night.

Imagine how my spirits plummeted once more when the teaching began and I saw Jetsun straining to read the small text. I had enlarged it, but not enough. On top of that, though I thought I had made it as large as the largest paper at the copy shop would accommodate, I saw that the lamas had cut the pages into strips. That meant I had not needed to fit more than one strip's contents on any page. I could have made the copies much, much larger. Despite my best efforts, instead of proving my competence I had failed at the only task Lama Pema had ever given me.

The next day I talked with Kaz again. Out of our discussion I came to see that I had been clinging to the idea of myself as competent and smart and that that was why Lama Pema had set things up the way he did. He had been willing to risk the success of the teaching for everyone just for the opportunity to help me grow towards freedom from my ego. I resolved that I would respond differently if given another chance.

Several weeks later I received a call from Michelle, Lama Pema's head student and the director of his New Jersey center. Lama Pema was supposed to be in New York teaching the advanced class that met all day Sundays, but he hadn't been able to leave the Jersey center because he had an important mailing that had to go out the following morning. She and Lama Pema had been up all night trying to complete it, but there was still a great deal of work left to do. As all the advanced students were in the class, there was no one to call to help except me. Could I come to New Jersey and help with the mailing so that Lama Pema could go teach his class?

I looked at the bus schedule and saw that a bus was leaving from the station a couple blocks from my house in another 15 minutes. She said she could pick me up at the bus stop on their side and thanked me profusely for the assistance.

Bear in mind that by the time I arrived Lama Pema was already about 3 hours late for the class he was teaching and still had to drive himself into the City. I found him at the computer, printing out announcements for an upcoming fundraiser for the Tibetan community. The event was soon approaching and the invitation to potential advertisers to sponsor the event was long overdue. I was to take over the printing job for him so he could go teach class.

In asking someone to print 200 copies of a file for you, it is likely that you would give a rather general instruction like, "Please print 200 copies of this file," and be done with it. That is regardless of how much of a hurry you may be in. There just isn't anything more to say. Yet Lama Pema managed to find 5 minutes worth of instruction on how I should complete the task.

It was only 5 minutes because that is how long it took me to feel the familiar contraction in my energy system that signaled I was about to resist something and decide to respond differently. At the 5 minute mark I gained enough perspective on myself to realize that I was feeling my intelligence questioned again and that my ego's defense mechanisms were kicking in.

I don't know if anything outwardly changed in my demeanor, since I had been agreeing with him from the start of his litany of instructions, but once I gained a clear view of myself within the situation I felt something soften within me and the idea dawned within me that it was okay if he thought I was an idiot. I knew I was a pretty smart person, but not everyone had to agree with me. If I was an idiot to some people, so be it.

At the very moment this understanding dawned within me, Lama Pema stopped speaking mid-sentence, looked directly into my face as if he was searching for something, then stood up and left for class without another word. I had passed the test on my first lesson.

With his help, one of the incredibly dense, unyielding, suffocating concepts of "self" that had been controlling my life, gave way just a bit, and there was some space there. In that space, I awakened just a bit more to an awareness of my true nature as a reflection of something inexpressible that could never be captured by any label.

If you find a qualified teacher to help you let go of some of your layers of self identity, do not miss the opportunity. If you cannot find a qualified teacher, or simply cannot trust any person enough to consider them qualified, consider a therapeutic relationship with a psychotherapist. The therapist won't be able to muck around in your actual life situations the way a guru can, but they can still stir up quite a bit just within the treatment room.

Ultimately, it is incredibly useful to get help, especially if you aren't yet able to achieve a direct experience of your higher self. In the chapter on Spirit I will introduce you to the practice of channeling and help you to make contact with your higher self. If you can establish a clear connection to the realm of Spirit you will find many capable teachers there.

Some of you will find an intimate, concrete relationship with non-physical guides comes quite easily to you. You can probably do quite well on the path of direct ego-transcendence without human intermediaries. You can let your higher self manifest teaching situations for you and give you the guidance and insight you need within the situations to tap the lessons. But for some of you any relationship with your higher self or spirit guides will remain abstract.

If you are in that latter group, get help. Use a human intermediary to help you get to the point where you can go the rest of the way alone. Whatever you have to do, find a way to escape beyond the limitations of labels you have accepted for yourself and regain the chance to be fully alive. Find some way to surrender to something beyond your ego identity and reclaim your freedom.

Surrender your false belief in separation and find your true home within the great ocean of eternal bliss. Surrender your achievements and find blessings instead. Surrender your importance and find harmony and peace.

Above all else, as soon as you are able, surrender to your higher self and become your true self. Let your highest wisdom live this life. Listen to your higher self throughout each day and be willing to act in accord with its instruction instead of insisting on doing things your habitual way. Watch and see how that changes the outcomes that arise, infusing every corner of your life with Spirit's love and grace.

As we now enter the third section of this book, we are going to focus more on what you do, or get help doing, to achieve the consciousness of bliss throughout multiple areas of your life and stabilize there. Since bliss is your true nature, this work is mainly about clearing blocks to awareness of what truly is and focusing full attention on that purity of being so that it takes an increasing share of your lived experience. We will look at clearing these blocks, embodying your higher self, and awakening to bliss consciousness in the areas of body, mind, emotion, spirit, and habit. But first….

Try This For Three Days:

Who do you create yourself as for others? Have you ever noticed a tendency in yourself to essentially announce yourself wherever you go in an attempt to control how you are perceived by others? Do you wear designer labels? Do you drive a car that is more expensive than you can really afford? Do you insist on the Dr. being placed in front of your name or the Ph.D. being placed after it?

Maybe none of these specific labels attract you, but if you are like most people, there is some identity that you are constantly working hard to promote and defend. Within your worldly confusion, you don't really want to be seen with unconditional love. You want to be loved for your personality, talents, and acquisitions – what you call "who you are."

I know this sounds backwards to you. You may insist that you don't want conditional love. You know that such love is undependable and you want something better. However, look deeply and you will see that to you unconditional love is mostly just an attractive idea that has fallen into fashion in your crowd. You don't really feel its value.

To be honest, you are still very much engaged with the pursuit of conditional acceptance from those around you. Denial doesn't achieve anything. It's okay to accept yourself as you are now, even as you watch yourself grow and change. Someday you truly will be fulfilled by love from people who know nothing about you. You will not be suspicious of such love. You will not feel compelled to chase after everyone with all the details of your life in an attempt to get them to affirm your value because of those details. Someday unconditional love will be enough, but for now, witness both drives within yourself.

For the next three days get acquainted with the identities that you are putting so much energy into upholding. Move through each day with attention to how you are hoping to be seen within each situation.

When you are driving along, what do you imagine the driver behind you is thinking? Are you going too slow? Are you going too fast? Do they like your bumper sticker? When you arrive at work, what do you want people to think when you first walk through the door? When you speak at a meeting, how are you hoping co-workers will react to your opinion? How do these hopes or fears affect what you actually do or say?

Some of these situations will prompt attempts to do image control for you and others won't. Each person has their issues and fortunately none of us is self-obsessed in every area of our lives. The important thing is to find your issues. Once you find them, just watch.

Don't try to stop yourself from reacting the way you do. Don't criticize yourself for being so concerned with what others think of you. The objective is to simply look at the walls you have built to shore up your imagined self. Look at the energy you have going into trying to prove that you actually exist as a solid thing that can be called "good" or "smart" or "rich" or whatever. No judgments. Just look and see.

Do this for the next three days and see what insight dawns. When the cost of your self-imposed imprisonment becomes more than you are willing to pay, you will choose freedom. And you will be free.

7 HABIT

"When you think about freedom, you think as if you will be there and free. You will not be there; there will be freedom. Freedom means freedom from the self, not freedom of the self." - Osho

The desire to be free is a dominant drive within all beings. When we think of things that interfere with that freedom we usually think of outside forces, but the primary obstacle to freedom does not come from outside ourselves. It is our own mental habit that keeps us recreating the same conditions that have displeased us in the past. Who we are is limited primarily by our own unconscious conditioning.

There are two legs in the journey towards full freedom. In the short run it is incredibly useful to learn how to create habits that will serve our happiness (positive creation). We must gain freedom from the habit of creating negative outcomes for ourselves (negative creation). In the long run, we must gain freedom from habit itself. We must transcend all habits and move into direct, spontaneous communion with the present moment without any agendas.

In previous chapters we have looked at different facets of transcending habit, such as innocence and self-knowledge and in coming chapters we will look at using meditation and channeling as paths that take us beyond habitual living. In this chapter we will work with the natural habit making tendencies of the mind to develop the first type of freedom – the freedom to intentionally create a future that is better than the past. The first step along both paths is the same – resume control over your mind.

There have been many useful ideas presented in this book (and all the others you have read), but in order for you to take advantage of this knowledge you must be able to change how you respond to the situations of your life. Remember, it takes just 30 days to make a new habit and 6 months to make it take root. Though usually we think of this in terms of bad habits, the same applies to the formation of good habits.

During this 30 day period the practice is to develop skillful responses and reinforce those new responses through repetition. You must think, feel, and behave differently if you want to see new outcomes. Since action follows thought, change requires that you be able to direct your mind at will, using it as a tool instead of having it control you.

First Steps

Shri Shri Ravi Shankar once told me that the key to enlightenment is to go from unconscious incompetence, to conscious competence, to unconscious competence. Our normal way of relating to every new moment based on past experience is unconscious *in*competence.

The unconscious *competence* we are pursuing here is the habit of being fully embodied as our highest possible self, our Divine presence, so that its natural harmony and beauty effortlessly unfolds in our lives. We must overcome our "incompetent" habits, ones that lead to more suffering, and make a habit of living beyond them. In that state, positive creation happens all by itself. You don't try to do good; goodness just flows out of your every thought, word, or deed.

Note, however that Shankar recommends *conscious* competence as an intermediary step. In the short run, we have to deliberately work to overcome our negative creation habits that leave us feeling frustrated, incompetent, pessimistic, cynical, selfish, isolated and aggressively competitive. That has to end, and the sooner the better, so we work at it directly.

Along the way to *unconscious* competence it is useful to develop a habit of *conscious* competence. In conscious competence, we are still being deliberate about what we create, still choosing and acting rather than simply revealing our basic nature spontaneously, but at least we are making good choices.

In using the freedom provided by the witness POV to intentionally direct your mind's creative process instead of just letting old habits control your life, you would be reprogramming yourself to habitually respond to similar stimuli with positive creation instead of negative creation. That is immediately helpful.

Using the first key you would learn to manifest the fulfillment of your highest intentions so you see that you are competent, loved, and blessed – with even better prospects for the future. Using the second key you would learn that lifting others up makes you feel better than tearing them down. You would replace the addiction to winning above others with a proclivity towards celebrating a life of joy with others. Developing the habit of using these keys to happiness is an incredibly worthwhile endeavor, even as you keep one eye on unconscious competence as your highest goal. Let us look more closely now at the techniques you can use to create these good habits.

The three approaches to working with habit we will look at in this chapter are concentration, repetition, and overcoming habitual resistance.

Concentration Practice: Creating Useful Habits

Concentration practice is the most valuable method you can use to develop self-mastery. Only with well-developed powers of concentration do you have a choice over where your mind is focused You cannot help that volition causes this or that to arise in your thoughts, emotions or physical reality, but you can choose to redirect your attention at will. You can choose to interrupt negative thoughts and direct your attention towards positive ones. You can that is, if you can concentrate long enough to do it! Any of the exercises that follow in this section of the book can only be done once you have enough concentration skill to control where you place your attention.

Concentration meditation practice helps build the habit of being able to: 1) redirect thoughts away from old images arising from a former belief in separation towards those that perceive our true connectedness, thereby creating beneficial outcomes for everyone involved; 2) redirect harmful emotions towards patience, acceptance, generosity, enthusiasm for service to others, a commitment to fairness, and general goodwill towards others; and 3) return easily to the higher self's unity consciousness POV.

It is therefore the key to being able to use the tools in the first three chapters (the 3 keys to happiness), the mind chapter (awareness meditations), the emotions chapter, and the spirit chapter. It is the single most important skill you can build right now. You will find several practices you can use to build concentration in the next chapter on mind. Use them.

If you are to truly live free from the grip of destructive past conditioning, you must make a commitment to discipline and develop yourself instead of indulging old selfish habits. Concentration practice develops self-discipline.

Over and Over and Over

Repetition builds habits. Over time, repetition of any practice will build new habits. If skillfully chosen, these habits will support your ability to create positive outcomes in life and even your eventual transcendence of all habits, as you get used to the enlightened way of thinking, feeling, and doing and your perception simply becomes spontaneously enlightened.

While research has shown that it takes just 30 days to create a new habit, I have found that it actually takes far less time than that. It seems to me to take more like 3 days. That is why each exercise at the end of the preceding chapters recommended you try it for 3 days. But don't take my word for it.

For the next 3 days, decide to associate two seemingly unrelated events. For example, every time the phone rings say mentally to yourself "Hello again." Or perhaps you prefer an event you can more directly control the frequency of, since repetition goes by occurrences not days. You have to do a thing quite a few times if a habit will result in just 3 days. If your phone only rings a couple times a day you probably won't even remember you are doing the exercise by the time you hear that unfamiliar brrrring-brrrring.

Try instead associating picking up a familiar object, such as an ink pen, with the thought, "And now." I am intentionally choosing inane responses so that you don't program yourself with anything destructive such as a sense of impatience, expectation, or judgment.

The point of doing this is for you to become thoroughly convinced of just how malleable your seemingly intractable bad habits are. You can replace bad habits with good ones simply by frequently repeating the new desired response far more often than you would naturally perform the old response.

For example, if you have a bad habit of expecting the worst, consciously choose to direct your mind to thoughts about good things you would like to see happen in the future. When you wake up think about all the good things that are going to happen that day. Every hour throughout the day begin the hour with thoughts about things you like and how you expect to have more and more of those things in your life. End the day with thoughts of how wonderful the day was and how the next day will be even better.

If you really are a person with negative expectations (a pessimist) you probably think this is bullshit. "I'm supposed to expect the best. Yeah right. I would, only I actually know there is nothing good in my life and things just keep getting worse."

Please note that I did not instruct you to analyze your life every hour and accurately assess your chances for good luck. Instead I said to consciously choose to direct your mind to certain thoughts. Accuracy has nothing to do with it. You have plenty of habits already that are thoroughly ridiculous so one more won't kill you. At least this one will begin to shift your reality so that over time its truth begins to emerge. Think positive thoughts about the future long enough and you will discover a future that is increasingly bright.

Rinse, repeat. Do it over and over and over, whatever the desired habit. Do it more than you normally perform the habit you want to leave behind. Over time one habit will simply get a leg up on the other so that the weaker habit dissipates into a vague memory of a distant, less fulfilling past.

Overcoming Resistance

Almost everyone has some degree of low self-esteem that can make it difficult to do what they know is best for them. When we are sabotaging ourselves we are not just saying, "Yes," to defeat; we are also saying, "No," to healing and growth. We are at odds with ourselves, unable to overcome our own resistance and create lives reflecting all the beauty and joy we desire and otherwise know how to create. Learning how to work with inner resistance to growth and change is one of the most valuable skills anyone can develop in life. Here are a couple of techniques you can use.

When I was a child, I used to give myself habits just for the sake of proving to myself that I could break them. I remember the last time I did it. I created a ritual of saying "Another one," each time I cracked my knuckles. After three days of it, I was hooked. It took me four days to get myself to stop! But I did stop.

Doing that strengthened my ability to not only break habits, but control my behavior at will in other regards as well. I share it with you now to suggest that you do something similar in terms of relating to your habits of resistance. Experiment with developing resistance to certain objects or ideas then dropping the resistance at will.

Pick any random object to which you attach no real judgment. Look at the object and think negative thoughts about it until you are able to feel a sense of repulsion arising in you. Once you really feel negative feelings towards this object, decide to drop the resistance. Now as you look at the object, think of the things you like about it. Do this until you feel your sense of repulsion replaced by a feeling of affection or attachment. Recognize how insubstantial your aversions and attachments must be if you can flip them based purely on the content of your thoughts. Continue looking at the object while deciding to have no feeling towards it one way or the other.

In this way, practice being the master of your destiny.

Resistance Exercise 2

Within the course of your daily activities, watch your reactions. You will observe that you recoil at some stimuli (sights, sounds, people, and so on) and are open to others. Notice how it feels in your body when you are rejecting an experience. Is there a tendency to contract your muscles? What happens to your energy? Notice how your physical and energetic experience differs when you are in acceptance. Is there a sense of relaxation, lightness, or even expansion?

You may find that contrast helps to highlight your reactions so that they are easier for you to see. If it seems that you are never able to be aware of the fact that you are reacting, let alone what the reaction is, add a little mental repetition to your experiment. As you go about your day, mentally repeat the word "Yes" over and over. No matter what you encounter, whether a field of flowers or a pile of horse manure on the road, just keep thinking "Yes."

Take note of when the "Yes" feels true and when it feels false. When it feels true, what do you experience in your body? When it feels false, what happens within you then? What effect does your contraction have on the situation you are rejecting? Does it improve things in any way?

Is it possible for you to switch from a rejection response to an acceptance one, just by choosing to do so? What happens when you successfully make such a choice? How does a sense of relaxation and openness within you affect your experience of the undesired stimuli?

The purpose of this exercise is for you to learn firsthand the cost of resistance to the present moment and the blessing of surrender to it. Judgment of the present is self-defeating. Only the future can be decided. The present is for action, preferably joyful action.

Habit lives in the past, ignores the present, and limits the future. The higher self makes choices about what it wants for the future, often communicating these choices to other parts of you through the same physical responses you use when you are judging something. The difference is, the higher self only discriminates when it comes to future creation, responding to your creative thoughts about the future with either encouragement or warning. It does not judge the present. It knows to never resist present experience.

In responding to the present with acceptance, alertness, and clarity about what is desired next, you get to use the present to create a future that reflects your fullest joy, peace, and well-being. Instead of being a reactive creature of habit, you get to be a fully alive expression of divinity playing with different aspects of itself, forever curious, eternally new. This is really the fundamental teaching of this book. Create good habits.

To achieve the greatest bliss possible in human life, all you have to do is create a habit out of choosing to live from the point of view of unity instead of that of separation. All around you, consciously choose to see peace not conflict, love not fear, freedom not victimization, friends not competitors. Choose like this again and again until it becomes an unconscious habit for you to see peace, love and freedom within community. Once you see it, you will be it.

Throughout each day, make it your top priority to practice bliss consciousness. Get good at it. Then you are literally home free.

8 MIND

There is a stillness at the center of all things. The whirling mind has an eye within its storm and entering there, you may rest. It is always there, ready for you to enter in. This chapter is here to help guide you to that resting place.

It is my most sincere desire that you should apply yourself to the practice of the meditations in this chapter with your greatest effort and full intent to see results. Not all of the meditative forms will work for you. Some are put here for others, but there will be at least a few that have a noticeable effect on you and at least one that can lead you to freedom if you keep at it long enough.

Consistency and perseverance are the most important qualities you must have if you are going to master your mind. Only once you master your mind is there any possibility of your being able to apply yourself to any other exercises in this book – or any other book, for that matter. If you can master your mind, you can skillfully work with the many personal growth tools available to you and craft a life according to your highest intent.

It is the nature of the mind to create unhappiness. Restlessness, regret, obsession, judgment, worry, control –

these are all normal daily fare for the mind. That is because it resists the one source of true happiness, the present moment. The mind goes to the past and future naturally in an attempt to live in a reality it thinks it can control. It dissects the past and plots for the future. It lives in fantasy if it altogether gives up on controlling the external world.

Most thinking is out of an attempt to control the future. Thinking doesn't happen in the present as anything more than perception. With that perception there isn't even judgment, just aware reception. The key to finding the joy, peace, love and beauty you desire to have around you is to first discover it within you. Stop making things up and just receive knowing. Pay attention to what is within you already and discover yourself. Relax and open to an experience of your full self and discover the world anew.

The aim of wisdom is happiness. If knowledge does not bring about happiness, then it is not wisdom; it is just information. Meditation is a method you can use to gain the most useful knowledge – knowledge of yourself and through yourself of the world around you. The level of intimacy you develop with yourself marks the limits of how intimately you may know the Divine. You cannot keep out only the dark. Ignorance of yourself means ignorance of all that is.

In manifestation work you can use concentration meditation to calm the mind (create a field of peace) or control the mind so that you can have a clear, stable visualization. You can also control your mind to interrupt thoughts that arouse disturbing emotions and take a step back to get some perspective on the emotions, rather than letting them carry you away. Concentration meditation practices help develop mental discipline, thereby giving you the power to choose where you place the energy of your attention.

A focused mind will help you overcome past habits so that you are available for new levels of bliss in your life. The degree of bliss consciousness you can embody depends on what you are doing with your attention. Concentration is a type of presence, determining how fully your energy is focused in the present moment rather than being dragged down by past conditioning or being obsessed with the future.

Insight/Awareness meditation practices are a little different. They do not replace concentration meditations, which are simply an indispensable part of personal growth, but they are an important growth tool as well. Insight meditation practices help develop self-knowledge and thereby wisdom. They tend to be more advanced practices.

Concentration paves the road to happiness and awareness is the cart that carries you down that road. Together they offer you freedom from the tyranny of a mind that has gone mad <u>and</u> taken over control. So make the road and take the road. Here is how:

<u>Logistics</u>

Often when meditation is taught the instructor will tell the students to practice for at least 20 minutes, twice a day. That is not my approach. Experience with numerous students has taught me that five minutes a day is a fine start, if that is all you can manage. Five minutes 3 times a day is my preference for beginners. If you have never had a daily meditation practice, I would encourage you to start with that goal. Spend five minutes doing the method right after you wake up, right after you come home from work or school, and again just before going to bed.

Once you have committed to a particular meditation practice, but are still in your first 30 days, expand to 10 minutes three times a day. You can pick whatever three times you want, but be consistent from day to day.

After the first 30 days are up and you are ready to make meditation a regular part of your life, see if you can go to one 10 minute session and one 20 minute session each day. Later expand to two 20 minute sessions daily. Many people eventually settle at one 30 minute session in the morning and one 30 minute session in the evening.

You may now be thinking, "An hour a day? I can't sit there watching my mind for an hour a day. I have things to do!" Hold on there, Nellie. I am not recommending you sit for an hour a day. I am recommending you give yourself 5 minute respites, sprinkled throughout your day, in which you stop the madness within you. Just pause a few times each day and be within yourself.

You will expand the sessions over time because you will find so much peace and joy within those precious minutes that you will want more. I give the progressive description of how your practice periods may lengthen so that you don't push yourself too quickly. It is not a demand that you do more, but rather an admonition that you do less. Gradual expansion is the key to maintaining the joy of the practice. If there is no joy in the process of creating the effect, there will be no joy in the experience of the effect either. The product will always match the process that created it.

As a final note before going on to the meditation techniques, I want to emphasize the difference between "meditation" and "meditation practice." While in normal conversation I and most others will use the term "meditation" to refer to the techniques we use in a meditation session, really the term "meditation practice" would be more appropriate. Meditation is what happens in the gaps within the practice. It is the stillness at the center of all things which we discover under the right conditions.

Please keep this in mind as you read further and do not be too rigid in your interpretation of the terms, since for ease of reading I prefer to use the term "meditation" many times when I am actually referring to meditation practices. With this understanding, let us now look at a variety of practices you can use to develop conditions conducive to meditation's spontaneous emergence.

Concentration Meditation Practices

Grounding Meditation

Whenever I feel a little top heavy with too much energy in my upper chakras, I like to do this meditation. I slow down my breathing while moving my attention from one foot to the other. This is especially good when meditating seated in a chair where your feet are flat on the floor.

To do the meditation in this manner, as you breathe in you think "left" and let your attention go to your left foot. As you breathe out think "right" and let your attention go to your right foot.

Continue to do this for the amount of time you have decided in advance. Do not let anything disturb your meditation, not background noise, not pains in the body, not flies – nothing. Set your intent to do a certain amount of time then fulfill that decision come what may.

Keeping your promises to yourself and breaking the tyranny of your wild mind is more important than avoiding a mosquito bite. You've been bitten before, but have you known lasting peace yet? This is a method to develop mental peace, a prerequisite for which is a calm and steady mind. It is a very useful meditation technique.

Mental Calming Meditation

This is one of the simplest meditations and most frequently taught. It is also the one that I have used the most over the 20 years I have been practicing meditation. Simplicity should never be underestimated. In this meditation you simply count your breaths.

The most basic technique is to think "one" as you breathe in, "two" as you breathe out, "three" as you breathe in again, and so on, up to a predetermined numeric limit. Six, ten, and twenty-one are all frequently used limits. When you reach the limit you start over again at one.

There are a number of variations on this theme. You could count independently of the breath cycle. That is useful if your mind is so jumpy that you lose focus between 5 and 6, or even around 2 and 3. Just count faster. Keep the breath slow and easy though – so don't try to count breaths if you need to speed up. Just count and don't concern yourself with the breath cycle.

When you have a fairly stable mind you can count complete breath cycles. You breathe in <u>and</u> out, then think "one," and so on. Try all three techniques and see which one most naturally fits the pace of your mind. Likely you will find that the appropriate technique fluctuates from day to day. When your life is more peaceful it is easier to concentrate, but when you are worried about something your mind will be more jumpy. Learning all three methods will allow you to pick the appropriate one when it is needed.

In any of the counting methods, if your mind wanders off you must start counting again at one and do not count higher than pre-decided limit. When you get to your limit, try to go back to one again without losing your concentration. This is not about counting to 1000. Actually, you are unlikely to reach even 10 if you are new to meditation, unless you cheat.

Remember, you must start over at one even if you think "meditation" thoughts like, "This isn't so hard." "I'm almost to 10 already." "I wonder if this is the right meditation technique for me." "Oh I can see the benefits of this." "I must not let myself be distracted by this passing car." All these thoughts are reasons to start over again at one, so don't cheat yourself.

And try to keep a smile on your face. When I teach meditation I notice a lot of beginners grimacing. They look like they are trying so hard to concentrate and not having any fun at all. Remember, the product will imitate the process that created it. I suggest you make meditation fun. Take a positive attitude about what you are doing. Smiling has a powerful effect on the emotions so it is skillful to use it.

One of the primary benefits of this practice, other than calming the mind, is that it trains you to be able to redirect your attention at will. Each time your mind wanders off you notice and send it back to its appointed task, which is the number one. Again and again, you stop yourself mid-thought and direct your attention at will.

It is important to be gentle with yourself in doing this. There is no reason to get mad at your mind for behaving the way all minds do until they are taught otherwise. When was the last time you watched a cartoon? Have you ever noticed how rapidly the image on the screen changes? That is because the cartoon's makers are trying to hold the interest of young children and they naturally have short attention spans.

But if you do an experiment with even adult dramas you will see that the image on the screen may be slower to change than in the cartoons, but it will still often fall around 3-6 seconds between a change of angle, distance, or subject. For any of these changes your mind has to scramble to reassemble an understanding of what it sees. It has to start over at one. The difference is that instead of doing a 20 minute daily meditation in focusing your mind so that it can eventually hold concentration for longer periods of time, TV watching is a 3 hour per evening meditation in jumpy mind!

So being as experienced as you are with "jumpy mind meditation" after all these years of TV viewing, do not be so hard on yourself. You should in fact be glad each time you catch your mind wandering off and get to send it back to one. It is giving you the opportunity to exercise your ability to redirect your mind at will.

This mastery of your attention is critical. In daily life you will often experience a pull towards focusing on the negative – on what annoys you, on what you lack, on people's imperfections, on what you don't want to have happen. In your meditation you will have been building up your power to redirect your attention at will, and so you will stop those destructive thoughts midstream and either refocus on the positive vision that you want to manifest, or simply recognize the illusory nature of what is arising. So there is no regret in getting lost in thought and regaining yourself during meditation practice. Starting from where you are puts you exactly where you need to be in order to face the challenges of your life right now.

Yoni Mudra

Yoni Mudra is a simple, yet powerful, ancient technique for turning within to find an experience of the source. To do it you close the sense organs to outside stimuli. You block off your over-active outer senses so that inner sensing can emerge into full consciousness. This is the easiest method to use in the midst of a chaotic life when your mental and emotional systems are over-taxed. It cuts right through.

As shown in the above diagram:

- Put both thumbs in your ears (either inside or holding down the outer flaps)
- Index fingers go on the eyelashes of your closed eyes to hold them down without pressing on the eyeball (hold lashes near the nose bridge)
- The middle finger rests gently on the nostrils, not yet closing them off, and

- The remaining two fingers press down on the upper and lower lip, holding the mouth shut and sealing the governing and central acupuncture meridians.
- Try to get into the position then proceed with the meditation technique itself. In essence you are using your hands as a vise across your face, pressing down on 3 key acupuncture points to dull physical sensation, silencing the audio stimulation that constantly pulls at your attention, withdrawing from visual stimulation as well, and focusing your awareness upon the breath, which I will explain next.

So in the meditation part you sit with your "face vise" on then:

1. Press down on the right nostril with the middle finger of the right hand so that breath can only come in through the left nostril. Inhale for a count of 4 (not seconds, regular 1,2,3,4) then close the left nostril so that both nostrils are closed and hold the breath for a count of 8.

2. Then leave the left nostril closed but release the right. Breathe out through the right nostril for a count of 16. You will have to exhale very slowly and gently or you will run out of breath before you reach 16. Without moving your fingers, breathe in again to a count of 4, now through the open right nostril.

3. Now close the right nostril also and hold the breath to a count of 8 ...

4. Repeat the cycle of alternate nostril breathing for as long as feels comfortable, but try for at least 5 minutes.

If you have a standard modern mind this is the way to do the practice. If your mind tends to be less active, you may be able to do a simpler breathing exercise and still achieve the result. Instead of counting inhales and exhales, just think that you are hearing the sound "sooooooh" as you breathe in and "haaaahhmmm" as you breathe out. You still close off one nostril and then the other, alternating which nostril breaths in and which breaths out and pausing with both nostrils closed in between. There is just no counting.

With either breathing technique, you will immediately notice the effects after you are done and open your eyes and ears. This is a very physical meditation practice. It stimulates the pineal gland within the brain, the physical correspondence to the 3rd eye within the energy system, and brings you fully into your present moment experience.

Insight Meditation Practices

The concentration meditation forms you just learned were concrete and precise. Insight meditation is more subjective. We are now talking about how you work with your mental perceptions and conceptions directly. Rather than controlling the mind, we are now seeking to learn from it.

Each method relies upon your contemplating the ideas presented, then watching for yourself to see that they describe what is happening within you. You do not take anyone's word for it. You come to an understanding of what I am claiming, then examine the situation firsthand. Once insight emerges, do not reach for the next thought. The mind will be quiet if real insight has been achieved. Rest in that still place of clear truth. This is the meditation.

You will have to develop some degree of mental concentration before you will be able to do any of these meditation practices since they require that you be able to watch your mind without getting carried away by your thoughts and forgetting that you are meditating. You are also going to have to sit to try the meditations before it will be clear what it is you are trying to do. Even then, it may easily take numerous attempts before you will have any clarity about what you see when you watch your mind. You will have difficulty separating the watched from the watcher. It will just seem like you are sitting there doing nothing.

The mind has a curious habit of being quite still when you first decide to watch it. Say to your mind, "Go ahead. Jump around like a wild monkey. I will just sit here and watch you." You will notice that it will not move. Then say,

"Be still now," and it will want to run all over the place. This is because it wishes to remain in control.

The concentration meditations are how you resume control. Once you have some success with them, add these practices to your repertoire as well. If you are a seasoned meditater you will find great benefit by adding these practices. Even if you are new and your mind isn't very stable yet, try each of these once so you can get a flavor for them. You will then be more likely to come back to them later once your concentration skills have developed.

All Sides Meditation

Within this meditation you are not fully outside your experience. You are not detached. You are aware of whatever experience is there. So if you are angry, you feel the heat and contraction of the anger in your body. If you are in love, you feel the euphoria and lightness. If you are breathing, you feel the air moving in and out. You stay in the body and are aware of the most subtle levels of the body's experience.

The key to this meditative form is that you do not let yourself get lost within the body's experience just because you are aware of it. Awareness is not full immersion in one point. You do not identify with what is being experienced as if it was who you are.

Feeling anger, you do not say, "I am angry." Instead you realize, "Anger is there within experience." You feel the anger and you know that it is arising from somewhere, that it has a stimulus and is not the whole of existence. It has not taken you over and become who you are. It is simply some part of what is emerging at that moment. There are always many things there, but some have a tendency to steal attention from all else, anger being a prime example.

You can also use breathing as your focus of awareness. Many people cannot have any perspective on their anger, because it thoroughly takes them over. It is a very strong emotion. Breathing is something people take much more lightly. You generally do not make yourself breathe. Most breathing just happens. Occasionally you become aware that you are breathing, but mostly it's beneath your awareness.

Watch your breath. You will observe that it is being caused by something, but this "something" is not your conscious mind. If you don't think to breathe in, the body still does so when it needs air, but if you do think about it, if you watch it, it still happens. Breathing is being caused by something outside your awareness. Yet you can fully experience the breathing from within it and can fully experience awareness of it from an outside point of watching breathing happen too. You know you are not controlled by breathing. You can hold your breath whenever you choose, even if only for a moment. You can temporarily stop your breath (or anger once you master it) even though you are not causing it.

In this way, you can recognize that you exist at multiple points within breathing. Something within you is causing breathing to arise. Since it is within you, it is part of you and therefore you are partly it as well. And something within you is doing the breathing. Your body is expanding and contracting its lungs and diaphragm so that air moves in and out. Something within you is also watching breathing happen. Your intellect is focused on this now because you are trying to watch your breath. So now you exist at a minimum of 3 points within breathing. You are the breather, the breathing, and the cause of breathing. If you watch long enough you will also discover that you are the breath.

Watching your breathing is the easiest entry point for recognizing that you are a being who exists at multiple points. You could also watch your mind thinking. Where do these thoughts come from? If you can watch your thoughts without getting carried away by the stories you come up with, if you can keep some perspective and not forget that you are watching the story and not living it, then clarity will arise. You will see that these thoughts are coming from somewhere and that you don't have to cause them. They arise seemingly all on their own. First you were watching your breath, but now you are receiving an award for being the best meditation teacher ever to live. Where did these ideas come from?

The mind has a strong momentum to its thought patterns. Your mental habits are well developed by the time you are old enough to buy a book like this one. So I know in speaking to you that you are running a lot of old tapes in your mind, day and night. If you just sit there and watch your thinking happen you will see one thought leading into the next without any direction from you saying, "First I will think about what I am doing right now, then I will lose awareness of what I am doing and begin to think about something that happened long ago; before I get to the end of that recollection I will be grabbed by a thought of someone in my current life who needs to learn the same lesson, which will transition into a plan to teach the world." And so on.

The habit pattern of the mind directs the whole episode, frame by frame, making it up as it goes along. And you get carried along for the ride because you have no perspective on what is happening. You believe that because you are thinking, it must mean you are the thoughts.

Imagine if you thought you were nothing more than breath simply because you constantly breathe. "Well," you would say, "I must be breath, because there is always breathing going on." That would seem pretty foolish, wouldn't it?

Yet you take the same stance towards your thoughts (and strong emotions) all the time. You get lost in your thoughts and forget that thinking is happening, that something is causing the thoughts, and that they will change without any prompting from your intellect.

And if you have a peaceful moment, the thoughts will even stop briefly. Then you will experience the ground of stillness within which the thoughts arise. That is the real meditation, but let us return now to the practice of meditating, since that is all you can direct. Meditation will sometimes arise if you do the practice, but you cannot make it happen so there isn't much point in going on about it within the context of instruction.

What I am describing here is taught in some traditions as Insight meditation practice. You watch your thoughts arise with the viewpoint that acknowledges that you are not the one causing them to arise. They seem to arise on their own. This separates you from the myopic perspective of everyday thinking so that there is an opening, a chance for insight to occur. The insight we are after is your awareness that you are all over the place. You are in fact everywhere. You are the thoughts to some degree, but you are also the reactive habit of thinking that causes the thoughts to arise, the mind that is experiencing the thoughts, the meditater who is watching the process, and the ground of stillness in which it is all arising. You are all of that.

I cannot convince you. I can only attempt to entice you. It must only make enough sense for you to try it. Sit down and watch something happen there within you. Watch your breath if you are a beginner and you want to be successful. Watch your thinking if you are already a great multi-tasker and can hold multiple thoughts in your mind at the same time. If you are more of a concentrative person who tends to get lost in one thought, better to use the breath.

In daily life it is useful to use the emotions. It is a great accomplishment to be able to watch an emotion arise while realizing that it is arising, that there is a cause for it arising, that it is not all of who you are even while it is a dominant part of your experience, and that part of you is watching the whole thing occur without having the experience of the emotion itself. The watcher isn't angry, afraid or sad. What is your watcher like?

Mine is blissful, always slightly amused, and extremely curious. Do you recall a time in your childhood when that could have described your general way of being in the world? So then you see what we are on to here. We are in pursuit of your lost innocence so that you can once again greet the world with freshness, vitality, wonder, and delight.

Follow your experience from multiple viewpoints. Let yourself be aware of being all that you are while engaged in the act of being it. Whether breathing, thinking, feeling, walking, bathing, eating – be fully there, from all sides. Discover your wholeness. Once you touch it, pause for a moment. Rest within the Self and savor the expansiveness and joy of fully being you.

Prajna's Meditation

They call me the Goddess Prajna Paramita, the Mother of all Buddhas, for I am the infinite, empty womb from which they were all born.

For thousands of years, numberless beings have worshipped Gods and Goddesses, but there is no initiation into my practice.

Crawl into my infinite, luminous womb and give birth to yourself.

What is self? What is Goddess? What is I or you or the space between?

Concepts.

Like air and wind and all that is constantly moving.

But there is a Truth beyond all of that.

It is everything ... and nothing.

No sight. No sound. No eyes. No ears. No body. No mind. No suffering. No path out of suffering. No confusion. And no enlightenment.

Within the stillness at the center of your being there lies a wisdom that has gone completely beyond.

> *Gate gate paragate parasamgate bodhi svaha*

I am within you.

You can find me easily in 3 places.

When you are seeing, look for me at the 3rd eye center.

When you are touching, look for me in the heart center.

When you are breathing, look for me in the pause between breaths.

When you find me, do not think about me. There is no use for inner conversation. Just relax and float within me without any mirrors. Watch, but be the watching, not the watcher. You do not need to see yourself when you are being yourself.

This meditation is the heart of meditation to me and is really three different meditations. In all three, you are placing the mind at two points so that a third point arises, then resting within the universality, clarity and peace of that third point, which is Prajna's womb.

She says, "When you are seeing, look for me at the 3rd eye center." If you are a mental sort who has a hard time stopping your compulsion to think, maybe even lying awake in bed at night because you just can't stop your mind, this is the method for you. Instead of getting lost in your thoughts, "seeing" from the perspective of someone inside the thought, step outside the thoughts.

Thinking is still allowed to happen so the mind won't fight for its life. As destructive as it may sometimes be, your mind is just trying to do what it believes is best for you. It has been taught that you will suffer and die if it doesn't stay on top of the things, so really it is just trying to care for you in its own special way. Even as you are grateful for this, you must find a way to break its tyranny or you will never know any peace.

So you are letting the mind perform its function. Meanwhile, you simply focus your eyes on the spot between the eyebrows, about one inch deep from the surface of your face. You focus your attention there. When she says "look for me" she means focus your awareness with alertness. Pay close attention to see what occurs. That is all. Just focus there. Look and see and keep on doing that even while your mind does its thing. The rest takes care of itself if you can be patient and attentive.

If you do this when you are very tired, you will probably fall asleep, which is exactly what you need most at that time. You can use the method for treating insomnia, but also try it during times of the day when you are more alert. If you find you are always falling asleep when you do this exercise then you are not being alert. You are not keeping enough distance. Step back a bit and remember that you are watching this happening, not letting it happen to you or fully being the watcher.

Prajna cautions us about this when she says, "Watch, but be the watching, not the watcher." If you get lost in the thoughts you are watching you will forget you are meditating and it will become just another "thinking" session with your mind mulling the same thoughts again and again and coming to the same dead ends again and again. If you can become aware of the watcher you will experience peace. But if you become identified there and become lost in that, you will fall into mental indolence. Your mind will become sluggish and will seem to float away. That is why you will fall asleep.

It will feel good if you normally experience a lot of tension and so you won't want to pull yourself out of it, even as you feel it happening. But just recognize that you are choosing between sleeping and awakening as your true self. You cannot sleep 24 hours a day. You must get on with life. Here is a technique you can use so that all 24 hours can be lived in peace. Do not miss the chance. Stimulate your mind enough to pull out of the position of watcher just enough so that you can watch the watcher. Watch the point. Watch the watcher. And thereby be the watching.

Or if you are an emotional person, "When you are touching, look for me in the heart center." Become aware of the area around your heart, the heart chakra, whenever you are touching anything or anyone. Very simple. Just place part of your awareness within whatever you are doing but reserve some of your attention for feeling what is going on in the heart. Do not try to feel anything in particular. Prajna is not saying, "love everything." You are likely to eventually discover that you actually do love everything, but she is not saying to try to make that happen. She just says, "look for me." That is all. Just look at the heart's experience, feel it, and see what is there when you are touching anything.

Your challenge will be to not get lost in the feelings. You must keep your mind alert. Just because the mind is a tyrant, that doesn't mean it doesn't have some good use. It is actually the most useful tool in your birth kit. Only through the mind can you achieve awakening.

The dog feels. It is very loving and can sometimes be sad, angry, all sorts of feelings arise. It is a master of feeling. Whatever is there is fully there for the dog, but where is its self-awareness? Is it able to see itself and make choices about how it will develop? Prajna is self-aware, and if you are to be one with her you must be self-aware too. So do not get lost completely within the feeling at the heart center. Just touch it so that you find her, but keep some perspective.

If you do this properly, you will experience a sense of oneness with whatever you are touching. You will recognize that all separations between "you" and "other" are mere concepts. We can usefully think about "you" and "it" and "me" and so on, so that we can consider the relationships between the parts. But the whole is also there and can also be usefully experienced.

If you like to take the universal road, the one most frequently traveled, the wide road, then Prajna says, "When you are breathing, look for me in the pause between breaths." You are breathing in. There is a slight pause. You are breathing out. Then there is a longer pause. You are breathing in again. And so it goes, every minute of your life. There is ample opportunity to find Prajna. Look for her in any minute of your life.

You breathe out and pause before breathing in again. This is natural. You don't try to do it. Let your awareness focus on that brief moment in which you are neither breathing in or out. In this whole life, such a tiny fraction involves not breathing in or out, just being there without any motion. Savor that precious stillness. Focus your full attention on it. Then let it go. When it comes around again, notice it again. Look into it deeply each time it arises, then let it go as it disappears into the next breath. Do not cling to it or anticipate its return.

If you do this, patiently and with full attention, you will discover an inner experience of peace and clarity. Eventually you will come to feel as though you are one with all of creation. You will be everywhere at once. You will be Prajna.

She promises this when she says, "You do not need to see yourself when you are being yourself." There is to be no separation between what is experienced within the stillness and who you are. It is you. You are what you are looking for and it is only you that can be found.

Mental Obscuration Meditation Practices

Jumpy Mind Meditation

Watch television.

9 BODY

You are like the wind. You can only be seen through your effect. You believe that you are this body, but you are not this body. Your body is a special effect. It is only special because you believe it is who you are. It is not who you are. You are Spirit reflected in a mirage of human form. Your body is the infinite stillness made visible through the cosmic dance.

Shamans open the portals between the spirit and physical worlds so that those energies merge and harmonize. I think of it as dancing God down to Earth. Any method you use that allows your higher self to take over your body for a little while and move it according to Spirit's whim, is the shaman's magic at work. That is the act of opening the pathway back home. And you are a natural shaman, whether you are using those abilities or not.

Community shamans open the portals so wide that everyone nearby is drawn in. Their journey into spirit is a shared one, usually with the intent of giving others access to cosmic sources of healing, rejuvenation, or wisdom. Long before you develop your abilities to that degree you can also use the shaman's art for self-healing, personal rejuvenation, and to access flashes of insight about your own life, among many other benefits.

There are two such methods that I will introduce in this chapter. The first is Ascension Yoga. It is for people who like to move more slowly with focused attention on the subtleties of what they are doing. The second is Ecstatic Dance. It is for you wild men and women with hyper-active minds who are never able to sit still for meditation, nor even bear the focused calm of yoga.

By practicing either or both of these methods you will be using the body as a part of your path of growth through joy. You will be bringing awareness of your naturally blissful higher self more fully into every cell of your body. Combined with a healthy diet that is low in sugar, over time these practices will leave you glowing as a radiant expression of Divinity in human form. Your touch will send joyful tingles down people's spines and your embrace will comfort the weary. Perhaps most fun of all, you will feel the nectar of bliss coursing through your veins whenever you pay attention to it.

The Basics

You should be familiar with the following three terms before we address the methods for the two movement practices presented in this chapter:

Chakras - rotating vortexes that exchange energy between the outer world and your spiritual, physical, emotional, and mental bodies. See the illustration below for the locations of the 7 chakras that are contained within the physical body. (Some chakras are located above or below the physical body.)

Each chakra conducts the flow of a particular form of energy. For example, the first chakra includes survival issues and the third chakra includes issues related to personal power and the ability to receive Divine Grace. Since concepts related to the various roles of the chakras are not worked with in the two practices being taught here, I won't spend time describing that, but I encourage you to make a study of the chakras elsewhere. Chakra clearing and balancing is an important part of my work with clients and makes a good part of a daily energy routine.

Sushumna - The energy channel that runs along your spinal column from tailbone to crown. The seven chakras lie at intervals along this column.

Shavasana - A resting pose in yoga. One lies flat on the back with legs a little more than shoulder width apart and arms out to the side, palms up. This is the final step in both practices and includes a meditative attention to the overall experience of being in your body. The mind is relaxed in the final shavasana. One does not get lost following after any particular thought, but watches the flow of thoughts and sensations as if watching a very realistic movie.

Awareness of the chakras and the sushumna column is an important part of both Ascension Yoga and Ecstatic Dance. Remember, the focus of the movement practices is to bring an awareness of spiritual energy more fully into the body. Since the chakras and sushumna are the conduits for this energy's primary movement into your individual energy system, attention to them can be the easiest method of observing the flow of spirit in the body.

The final shavasana pose creates space for you to integrate the benefits of the preceding practice. Within the mental field this integrated energy takes the form of inner peace. Within the emotional field it is a sense of being embraced from within by love. Within the physical field it is relaxation of all tensions, and within the spiritual field it is the presence of the higher self and its natural witness consciousness.

Since both these spiritual practices involve physical exercise, you should check with your doctor before beginning, especially if you haven't been exercising regularly. Just because it's spiritual, doesn't mean it can't hurt you. You should feel good while you are doing the practices, not like you are straining. At the end you should feel exhilarated, not exhausted.

The Ascension Yoga Practice

What is Ascension?

If we use a metaphor to describe spiritual reality wherein "up" represents wholeness, or closeness to God, and "down" represents fragmentation, or separation from God, we can then speak of the return to Unity consciousness as "Ascension." As we ascend, we are climbing the metaphorical staircase towards wholeness. The return is an illusion of course, since the original departure was like a dream. The idea is to work within the dream constructively to get yourself to a level where you can awaken from it and realize you were always fully embraced as part of the whole.

What is Ascension Yoga?

The idea for Ascension Yoga came to me while I was channeling during the Shavasana pose of what was then my daily Sivananda yoga practice. I studied Sivananda yoga for several years, including study at their ashram in India, and adapted it to my personal needs over the years. So I was doing this adapted practice, actually.

As I lay there observing the flow of subtle energies in my body and watching it affect each chakra, I heard one of my spiritual guides saying, "Ascension Yoga." It then hit me like a flash that the channeling, bodhicitta (universal compassion), chi, and Kundalini work I normally do as part of my personal spiritual growth practice was actually folding into my yoga practice so that the yoga was a part of my ascension work. It then occurred to me that others might benefit from guidance in adapting their personal yoga practices in a similar manner. So I decided to develop the method more formally and offer it to others.

Ascension Yoga is meant to be an adjunct to an existing yoga practice. It is a method of approaching any type of yoga so that it serves your personal, and thereby planetary, ascension. It is by no means a substitute for actual yoga instruction. If you have never done yoga before I suggest you take a few classes, or even a few courses, before trying the Ascension Yoga practice – so that you don't hurt yourself trying to get into the asanas.

Alternatively, you can use any standard stretching positions you are familiar with in place of yoga poses (asanas). Just remember to breathe steady and deep while in each stretch. The point is to use the technique while letting the body move into whatever form it wants, while applying meditative awareness.

Benefits of Ascension Yoga

The awakening process of Ascension Yoga is gradual. As more and more of the unity consciousness of your higher self descends from crown to root chakra – cleansing, purifying and opening as it goes – more and more spirit energy is integrated within the root chakra. This integrated energy then ascends as the power to manifest the divine aspects of each chakra.

The transformation process is effortless and is carried by the pure being of the person, not by conscious intent. And it is not all or nothing. Traumatic Kundalini awakening experiences are not the aim of Ascension Yoga. We do not start with the seat of the Kundalini, but rather let the awakened consciousness reach it, releasing a gentle stream from the great river, as universal love is integrated within the full chakra system.

This method differs from Kundalini awakening practices primarily in that it begins from above instead of from below. The gradual awakening of Kundalini power is a result, not the aim of the practice. The spontaneous benefits which intensify as Kundalini gradually unfolds within the integrated chakra system are:

For Self	**For Others**
Physical health and vitality	Tendency to make those around you feel grounded and focused
Enjoyment of life	Creating a womb of safety in which the inner child of others is free to play in delight and develop self-confidence
Self-acceptance and self-understanding	Wisdom that makes others feel heard and guided at once
Abundance	Generosity
The ability to get one's point across easily and to connect with all kinds of people	Creative sound whereby the voice soothes, heals, encourages, and effectively instructs all that hear it
The ability to manifest visions of joy, peace, and love within all situations of life simply through visualization (and a habit of envisioning stories that reflect joy, peace and love)	Ability to bless others just by thinking of the desire that they be blessed
Union with the higher self and awakening as the true self	Tendency to bring others to an expanded consciousness when in one's presence

The Ascension Yoga Tenets

This technique is continually evolving as I advance with my own ascension work. It is meant to be an organic process and you are a part of its evolution. That means you should not try to force yourself into an exact replica of what I am teaching you here. The idea is to learn the vocabulary and tones then make up your own songs. Sing your true self and contribute your original melody to the symphony of being. Feel free to adapt the method for your own needs.
This leads directly to the first tenet of Ascension Yoga ...

Let the Yoga Move You

So many times yoga is taught as static poses handed down for millennia and the idea is to "get it right." In Iyengar yoga especially it is taught that the body most be perfectly aligned in the pose in order for the benefits to be had. Well Ascension Yoga teaches just the opposite, which is not to advocate sloppy yoga. The focus of attention, intention, and committed effort of traditional yoga must remain. But let your higher self speak to you and guide your yoga.

The order of the asanas, the duration they are held, whether they are static or fluid, minor alignment adjustments that suddenly free up torrents of energy ... all these things vary from person to person and from day to day. Imitation may be the most sincere form of flattery, but it is not the most sincere form of yoga. Be true to your yoga and it will serve you faithfully. Trust your innermost wisdom. You are, after all, one with God, are you not? Well God didn't cease to exist millennia ago. He/She/It is still active and available to you whenever you decide to direct your attention

Godward. Even right now. Go ahead and check to see if you don't want to take my word for it.

Which brings me to the second tenet of Ascension Yoga ...

Ask for Help

Set your intention at the beginning of the session that you wish to receive healing in alignment with your highest good. Ask Buddha, your higher self, your spirit guides, whoever you feel inspired to pray to, for support and guidance as you do your practice. Remind yourself of what ascension is about and become clear in your intent that all your actions, including the yoga, be a part of your spiritual awakening.

And lastly ...

Remember Love

"The Source" can be thought of as the union of bliss and emptiness. Emptiness refers to pure potential that can take any form, but has no static form. Bliss is the union of love, peace, and joy. The peace that arises when we let our bodies evoke emptiness by taking the many forms (poses) of yoga is well acknowledged. Even the joy one feels after classes or sessions is fairly well appreciated. But rarely do you hear mention of the love that is aroused in the practice. Yet love is the widest path to full awakening as our unique manifestation of Source energy.

Love for others. Love for oneself. Love without measuring, hording or compulsion, true love, is an aspect of God Itself. As you engage in your practice of Ascension Yoga, continually redirect your attention back to the sensation of love coursing through your veins and subtle energy system (meridians, flows, etc.). It is there. It feels like bliss. It glows and is warm and soft. It says, "Yes."

Watch it flow and drink it in. Love yourself and end your session with an announcement of your intention to take that love out into the world and share it with others. May you be an instrument of God's healing love, and His peace, and Her joy, unfolding in this world of infinite bliss.

In Summary, the 3 Tenets of Ascension Yoga are: Let the Yoga Move You, Ask for Help, and Remember Love. As long as your yoga embodies these 3 tenets, you may consider yourself doing Ascension Yoga. Now I will share with you my current technique for applying these tenets.

The Ascension Yoga Technique

There are 6 simple steps to the Ascension Yoga Technique:

1. Begin with 5 - 15 minutes of aerobic activity. This can be standard sun salutations, a few minutes on your exercise bike, anything that gets the blood pumping and forces the breath to deepen.

2. Move into Shavasana (lying flat on the back with palms up) for a minute or two and return to it between every few yoga asanas. Let your inner guidance signal when it is time to return to Shavasana. Within Shavasana REMEMBER LOVE. Feel it moving through you, healing and loving you as it goes. Before moving from Shavasana into the first pose of your regular yoga practice say a prayer to God, spirit guides, your higher self, whoever you would like to ASK FOR HELP in achieving the goals you are setting for this yoga session.

3. As you move through the asanas of your practice, LET THE YOGA MOVE YOU. Let your inner guidance choose

the order and duration of each asana. Each time you find the right balance within a pose, let yourself relax in that pose before moving on. Be aware of your chakras as you relax into each pose. Scan your sushumna (the channel of light that runs along your spine from tailbone to crown). Let your awareness move freely between the sushumna and the 7 chakras it contains, the sensations in the muscles being flexed in the asana, and the general overall feeling of being in your body. When the energy seems to stop flowing (when you are bored or the sensation of pain takes over your awareness), move back into Shavasana and prepare for the next asana.

4. Be sure to include one or two balancing asanas at the end of your practice. Notice how the stability of your mind affects your ability to stay balanced. When you feel yourself tipping over, focus your mind on a visible point on the horizon. Sharpen your concentration and you will see that your balance responds accordingly. This is more effective than trying to create balance just by controlling the muscles.

Move from the last balancing pose into these two movements from Chi Kung. These are done standing.

First, balance the left and right hemispheres of your brain. Do this by raising the right arm above your head while raising the right knee towards your chest to a comfortable height. Breathe in as you raise the right side. Then raise the left side in the same manner as you breathe out. Repeat for 3-5 breath cycles then switch to alternate side movements. Raise the left arm with the right knee and let both cross the body as you do this. It's sort of like walking in place with a really exaggerated motion. Breathe in when the left arm is raised this time, balancing the energies. Repeat for several breath cycles.

The second Chi Kung exercise brings more chi into the body. It is done walking in place or if you have space walking in a large circle around the room. Basically you will be moving energy into the solar plexus by gracefully moving your arms from right to left and left to right as you walk.

Start with both arms extended in front of you at stomach height, then sweep both arms to the right side as you breathe in 3 quick breaths and step down on your right foot. Then float the arms to the left as you breathe out one long, slower breath and step with your left foot. Repeat for 10 or more breath cycles.

As you do this you will notice that when you move your arms to the right your left hand stops pretty close to your center/side. The same happens with your right hand when you move both arms to the left. Become intentional about this movement now and imagine that you are pulling energy (prana/chi) into you solar plexus as the trailing hand moves towards your center. Aim for the solar plexus instead of letting the hand wrap all the way around to the side. See if you can imitate an infinity sign (doing a sideways figure 8) across your body as you move your arms from right to left and back again.

Practice doing the arm movements with just the breaths at first, then add in the walking movements once that is clear to you.

5. When you are done with the chi exercises, remember to return to Shavasana one last time. This time cover yourself with a blanket or put on a sweatshirt, even if you don't feel cold. Your body temperature will drop and you don't want to

use any of the chi you have just brought in trying to stay warm.

This time in your Shavasana do not focus on the flow of love, or energy, or anything else. Just be. Let the mind rest completely. This is the moment for which the entire practice has been preparing you. You are the union of bliss and emptiness, pure love, peace and joy that can take any form. Relax and let go, resting in pure being.

6. When you are ready to end the final Shavasana announce your intention that the powerful love you have generated in this session will be taken out into the world to raise the vibration of everyone you encounter. Thank God, your guides, and your higher self for their loving assistance and rise as the ascended master you truly are.

The Ecstatic Dance Practice

One of my earliest memories is of dancing around my living room with my Cherokee great-grandmother. I remember her clapping her hands as she shook her hips from side to side, her eyes flickering with an inner light and a slightly amused smile on her face. And I remember feeling free, bubbling with joy and completely safe.

While I was in the depths of depression years later I would draw upon that early teaching. Alone in my studio apartment, night after night, I would turn off the lights, turn on the music, and dance until my feet ached and pains shot up and down my shins, so that I had to finally fall onto my bed and just lie there, allowing the dance to continue within me. Dancing alone in the dark was the one bright spot in my life for many years and it was how I preserved my sanity.

As I began to emerge from my depression, dance continued to be a key part of my healing process. During my Master's program in Counseling Psychology I was exposed to dance therapy, including the work of Gabrielle Roth. Her work provided me with a vocabulary and history to give meaning to much of what I had spontaneously been doing to maintain some degree of emotional functionality. As an added benefit, I came to understand that there was more than one way to meditate.

My mind was too chaotic for meditation for all of my twenties. I couldn't even sit still for more than a few seconds at a time. Some part of my body was almost always moving, even if it was just my foot tapping or my facial expression changing. I lived in constant avoidance of myself. Consequently, I had to also avoid the stillness that would force me to face myself.

I was convinced of the value of meditation and had practiced it successfully during high school, but I thought I could no longer access meditation's benefits until I could get myself to sit still again. What do you do when you aren't calm enough to do the practice that is meant to help you calm down?

I couldn't control my wild mind. But through a combination of dance therapy forms I was learning in my Master's program and my own natural healing dance practice, I reclaimed my rights over one territory in my life – my body. I decided to take this body and offer it to Spirit. "Here I am," I announced to Spirit, "You may live here."

Since that time I have performed my "Spirit Dance" internationally and taught it to adults in Asia and children in New York. I surround the term in quotes because I don't consistently call it that or anything else. To me it isn't about labels or properties. I think of Ecstatic Dance the way you might say Jazz Dance or Modern Dance. It describes a whole school of movement styles.

The instruction that follows is my current way of opening the portals between Spirit and flesh so that I become a pure channel for wholeness moving within the fragmentary realm of matter. I do it because it feels good. I do it because it has become my habit to respond to music in this way. I do it as a moving meditation and practice of surrender and communal embrace. If you want to do it too, here is a way to begin.

What Makes it Ecstatic

There is more that differs between the practice of different ecstatic dancers than that which remains the same. Some people go deeper when they dance alone, because they are too self-conscious when they are being watched. They can't help but to try to perform and the desire to control the dance so that you appear a certain way is the death of ecstatic dance. You cannot serve two masters.

Some people do better in a group because the group helps them stay focused. Alone they would loose energy for the practice after a few songs. They would doubt the value of what they are doing and abandon it before its fruits ripened. There is also something really powerful created within a group of dancers if they are able to harmonize as a collective body of movement.

Some people will only dance to instrumental music because they are distracted by words. Others like to listen to pop music and are inspired by the upbeat messages. It is easiest to use music with simple, steady rhythms if you want to be able to "trance out," but any music can work if it makes you feel like boogying until you just can't shake it no more.

In a few pages I will offer you a specific approach to the dance you can use, but you should not feel limited to it at all. It is a starting place. After you journey in through there, over time you will discover your own way of bridging the realms. There will be yet another form of ecstasy in motion that is birthed through you.

Despite the many differences, what unites the forms of ecstatic dance and differentiates them from regular free-style dancing is the intention and the entrainment. The intention is to connect with the sacred realm and allow something unknown to emerge – not to look good, develop dance technique, impress people, or entertain your ego with ideas about channeling ancient spiritual dances from around the world. Save the "stories" about the beauty or achievement of what you are doing for when you are performing sacred dance before an audience. The intention in personal practice is surrender – and maybe even self-discovery.

Entrainment is the process by which the intention is fulfilled. By synchronizing the rhythms of the body with those of the realm of Spirit, the dancer is able to bridge the divide. A single pulse moves through you and all that exists, as you become the union of Spirit in matter.

For some people making the rhythms themselves is the most powerful way to enter the trance of the sacred communion. Those people drum, or play other rhythm instruments. But the interplay between the drum and the dance is just as fertile.

You surrender your body to the music, following the cosmic currents the musician has tapped and entering there. Pretend that you are having a conversation with the music, one without words. The music speaks through rhythm and melody and your body responds through motion and shape. Back and forth, back and forth, the music enters your body and the body gives form to the music.

Before long, you can let go of the music and ride the currents of inner sound directly. If you allow yourself to keep dancing after the music ends, dancing into the silence, you will discover that there is a symphony playing within you at all times. And it wants to come out. It wants to be seen. It wants you to breathe into it and give it form.

Watch yourself dancing. Focus so intently on the subtle urges within you to move this way or that way or not at all that you completely disappear inside the music and the dance. Concentrate as you move, directing full awareness at the experience that is occurring inside you. Be open to whatever comes through your body in the form of motions as you surrender to your higher self. Dance long enough and hard enough until your mind has no choice but to let go. Lose the dancer and be only the dance.

You will discover ecstasy. Play whatever music you want. Dance in the dark or behind covered windows. Do it in the day or night, with headphones if you are worried about disturbing anyone. But do it. Dance until you can't move anymore. Listen. Breathe. Move. Respond. Discover who you are as Spirit given shape as a body.

A Sample Ecstatic Dance Session

Here is a method of moving to get you started. Prepare as follows:

Lay out music in advance that you can use for each of the segments. If you have the technical abilities, consider creating a playlist or burning a compilation CD on your computer. The songs you will need are described in each step. Song lengths of about 5 minutes are good.

Make sure that you won't have to be concerned about anyone disturbing you, whether walking in, ringing the phone, or even just watching you from an adjoining room. You want to be able to enter your inner world with full attention, letting only the music, the breath, and the floor connect you to anything outside yourself.

Dance with eyes closed as much as possible, opening them occasionally for balance.

You don't need a lot of space, one square yard will do, but if you have room to skip, swing or glide around the floor, great.

Dance barefoot, unless you have weak arches.

Steps in the Practice:

Begin with a song that has a clear, steady beat. The simpler the rhythm the better. You will be using the first song to ground into your feet. Turn on the music, close your eyes, and begin shifting your weight from one foot to the other and back again. Let your arms hang loose at first but feel free to move them, and any other part of your body, if you are so inspired as your connection to the music deepens. Maintain awareness of your feet on the floor as you move and breathe full breaths. Be careful not to breathe so deeply that you feel spacey. The first chakra is being stimulated in this step.

The second song should be one that has a simple rhythm and a clear base line. If you aren't clear what a base line is, just think of music that feels funky, sultry and hip swinging sexy. You will be focusing your awareness on your hips during this song, letting the music pull you from side to side, back to front, round and round, with its rhythm and flow. Let the arms do what they like, surrendering the full body to the lead of the hips. The second chakra is being stimulated in this step.

The third song should be hard pumping so that your entire body goes wild with the dance. Thrash. Surrender to chaos and let it reveal itself through you. Don't try to control how you appear. Don't try to dance. Just move the body with abandon. This will stimulate the third chakra.

The fourth song should have a melody you enjoy. Focus awareness in the heart center and also be aware of movement impulses within the arms. Intend to have your arms express your energetic feeling of the music moving through you. If it is not too much mental activity for you to still feel the music, think of people you love or of self-love while you focus in the heart center and dance from your heart. If you are in a group, simply become aware of your feelings towards those around you without trying to make yourself feel anything in particular. The fourth chakra is being stimulated in this step.

For the fifth song choose something inspiring. Some people like choir music, others Irish jigs, maybe for you something whimsical and silly – whatever opens you up and makes you feel light and free. Focus your attention on your third eye at the center of your forehead as you dance, opening the two physical eyes now and then for balance. Think of you higher self and make the request that it merge with you as fully as it is able. Offer your body to your higher self now and watch it dance through your body as if you were a witness, not the dancer. The sixth chakra is being stimulated in this step.

Continuing dancing as your higher self for however many songs time allows. Choose whatever music makes you feel like dancing. Let your inspiration guide you. Make sure you have enough energy left after the last song to go on dancing as it trails off into silence.

Dance in the silence for at least 1 minute. If no movement comes, don't force it. Just stand still and wait, maintaining your focus on your inner experience and intending to let the higher self reveal itself through you. Surrender to even the most subtle impulses to move. Don't think about looking like you are dancing or looking like anything in particular. Move without making up mental stories about where the movement is going and what it is trying to say. You can reflect and analyze later if you want to.

End the dance practice by lying in shavasana pose for 5-10 minutes and letting your awareness drift freely. Thank your higher self for its assistance as you rise and express your intention to continue deepening the relationship in future sessions.

Remember, this sample class is meant to get you started. It is a template. Adapt your practice to what works best for you. If you are physically fit, add a few more songs in step three to extend the workout as much as your stamina allows. Just make sure you have enough energy left to finish the other steps and that you have fun from beginning to end.

Some great musicians to try out are Jai Uttal and the Pagan Love Orchestra, One Giant Leap, the entire Buddha Bar series, Afro Celt Sound System, Nomad, Gabrielle Roth and the Mirrors, Shimshai, and Deva Premal. For my private practice I mix in some popular music, such as Prince, Moby, Jurassic 5, Beyonce, Santana, and Ozomatli. The important thing is to use music that makes you feel like dancing and mix in at least a little that also lifts your spirit. It's okay to play with the shadow by using "darker" music like rap or heavy metal. Just don't make that the core of your practice.

Bliss in the Body

You are like an infinite Light reflected in the form of a human body. Anything you do to discover just how true that statement is will help you develop your habit of being bliss. Feeling good inside your body is an important part of being bliss. Many times when negativity overcomes me and I want to redirect my mind towards something that makes me feel good, I will simply tune-in to the experience of ecstasy coursing through my veins. I embody my spirit so fully within my flesh that often I can actually feel it there.

I want you to have this instant access to bliss too, so work at your yoga or your dance until you do. Then continue to do it because it's fun. Do it because it's the way to do any form of movement. Do it because you are living as embodied Spirit at all times and sometimes you just like the way it feels to move.

10 EMOTIONS

Recall that we spoke in the first chapter about the creative power of emotions. Consider what it means to live in a state of emotional turmoil. What are you creating?

Mastering your emotions is an indispensable component of mastering your destiny. The ability to surround images of what you want in life with a feeling of joy, peace and fulfillment is essential if you want to be able to use manifestation skills to your advantage. The ability to calm your emotions so that you can receive intuitive guidance from Spirit is also crucial.

Intuition is the method your higher self uses to communicate with your conscious mind. Through intuition your higher self tells you what actions you can take right now to help you realize your most meaningful and expansive goals. The two greatest obstacles to your being able to hear and follow this guidance are mental resistance to taking direction (control issues) and emotional disturbances which cloud the information being received.

In the Habit chapter we looked at the issue of mental resistance and exercises you could use to overcome it. Hopefully you did the exercises and saw some increase in your ability to drop resistance at will. You probably also learned the emotional cost of mental resistance by seeing the tension and unpleasantness that came up whenever you decided to resist something. This clarity can give you the firm resolve you need to be willing to allow the wisdom of your innate being to emerge.

In this chapter we will focus on overcoming the second obstacle to receiving clear inner guidance – emotional disturbances. We will look at working with emotion in ways that allow the emotional tool to serve your happiness instead of undermining it.

Emotions such as anger, fear, attachment, envy, pride, listlessness, apathy, and sadness make it difficult to hear the wisdom of your inner guidance. They are therefore impeding emotions; they impede your development if left in place. They result from rigid patterns of disturbed energy within any of your energy bodies – physical, emotional, spiritual, or mental.

It can sometimes even be difficult to distinguish when emotional-sensory information is coming from the higher self or the patterns of stuck energy that generate impeding emotions. Both emotions and guiding intuition emerge into conscious awareness from the subconscious. The easy way to know the difference is to watch what happens when you process the information.

Intuition tends to get more clear when you sit with it, whereas emotion tends to resolve itself and disappear.

There are four highly effective approaches you can use to process information coming from your subconscious mind: 1) Private expression; 2) Relational expression; 3) Instant release; and 4) Delving for understanding.

Private expression - If a feeling is too strong to sit with and may even be causing physical problems, express it privately. Try art processes, journaling, yelling, or hitting a pillow or stuffed toy.

Relational expression - If the knowledge of a feeling would directly benefit another or benefit your relationship with them, express it to them.

Instant release - If a feeling can be sat with, but is preventing you from feeling your joy or hearing your inner guidance, release it on the spot.

Delving for understanding - If a feeling can be sat with, but it won't release, only growing more clear as you try, delve into it. It is probably your higher self trying to communicate with you – intuition.

In terms of private expression, there are many well known methods for cathartic release of emotions, so I won't try to cover that here beyond saying that I recommend that everyone keep a journal. Learning how to effectively communicate negative emotions to others is also an enormous subject so I will direct you towards the excellent work being done within the "Non-violent Communication" field if you want to develop those skills.

Over the years I have developed an emotional clearing technique I call Release Breath Method that I have found to be extremely effective in helping clients instantly release troubling emotions or clear them by receiving needed insight. The method grew out of my experience using a combination of Dr. Eugene Gendlin's Focusing work, cognitive therapy, breath-work practices, and meridian therapies within my clinical training, personal growth work, and professional energy-work practice.

I will present the shorter, cognitive method first since you would normally only go on to the longer method if you are unable to release whatever emotion is disturbing you and the feeling is getting clearer instead of dissipating. The longer, more comprehensive method for gaining insight can be used on persistent emotions that are more likely intuition insisting on communicating something of vital importance to you. It is also the method of choice when you feel a murky sense of something troubling you, but don't quite know what it is.

Release Breath Method uses the mental and physical bodies to create harmony within the emotional body and help you access your highest wisdom. If you channel, you will find that channeling flows much more easily after a 15-20 minute Release Breath session than if you start cold. In fact, when I teach Learn to Channel classes the first meeting focuses almost exclusively on teaching students the method.

Quick Emotional Release Method

This cognitive therapy method doesn't resolve underlying issues within the subconscious. Nor does it put us in touch with important insights that our inner guidance may be trying to share with us. However, not all emotion is the communication of guiding wisdom. In fact, most emotion is just habitual reactions that come from past wounding. It is dead energy that we are holding on to and that is draining our life-force energy. If there is nothing to learn from an emotion, the best thing to do is to just drop it. The following method will help you do exactly that. You may then follow it up by generating a positive emotion within you to support positive creation or by just resting in the place of peaceful clarity and enjoying a moment of complete emotional freedom. (Even positive emotions can be confining. True freedom means freedom from duality itself.)

Begin by re-acquainting yourself with a range of emotions. As you read each emotion on the list, generate the feeling of that emotion within yourself. Make sure you really feel it and are not just thinking about it. It may help trigger the feeling if you think of situations or people who tend to arouse that particular response in you. Thoughts are always what trigger emotion, however conscious or unconscious the thought may be.

Now feel bored ….

Feel disappointed ….

Feel worried ….

Feel insatiable (like you will never have enough of something) ….

Feel defiant ….

Feel angry ….

Feel smug ….

Feel enthusiastic ….

Feel confident ….

Feel generous ….

Feel peaceful ….

Were any of these emotions familiar to you? Where did you feel each one in your body? Think about other emotions that you sometimes feel. Which emotions play the most dominant role in your life?

Now that you have sampled a bit of the range of human emotion, you are ready to begin releasing your mental clinging to habitual emotional patterns. Start with whatever feeling is dominant in your awareness right now. Allow yourself to fully experience the feeling and appreciate its value with love. Then:

Examine – Cognitively examine the possibilities for how you <u>might</u> respond to the feeling. For example, could you let the feeling continue as it is? Is that possible? Could you let the feeling go if you chose to? Could you accept either having the feeling continue or having the feeling stop? What are the possibilities for how you could relate to this feeling?

Decide – Select what response you prefer and when you want to use it. For example, would you like to allow the feeling to continue? Would you like to let it go? Which will you do? When will you do it?

Let action arise spontaneously from within instead of resulting from any physical action on your part. If it is just mental habit that is generating the emotion in the first place, change can happen as soon as you decide what change you want and when you want it. Your clear intention is highly creative, particularly within your internal reality.

Repeat the process as many times as you need to until the emotion is completely cleared. You may notice that one feeling clears only to be replaced by another. Keep doing the process until when you ask yourself what you are feeling right now the answer you get reflects a sense of complete well-being. When the feeling is resolved, pause for a minute or two to savor the feeling of being free. The entire process (from examining to deciding) usually takes only 1-3 minutes. This method is the one you should use first when troubling emotions arise during the course of your life.

If the intensity of the emotion doesn't diminish as you do it – if you repeat the process 4-5 times and still feel the same or the feeling gets even more clear – you are dealing with intuition. In that case, you need to delve into the feeling more deeply to learn the lesson it is there to teach you. Find some time to do the full 15-20 minute Release Breath Method.

Release Breath Method

There are 12 steps in the full Release Breath Method:
1. Grounding
2. Breathing
3. Centering
4. Scanning
5. Selecting
6. Experiencing
7. Visualizing
8. Naming
9. Appreciating
10. Receiving
11. Acting
12. Savoring

Grounding – Close your eyes and draw your attention inward with the intention that you are going to learn and heal through this process. Take a minute to feel your feet on the ground or in some other way deepen your awareness of your connection to the Earth.

Breathing – Keep the energy moving by maintaining some attention on the breath throughout the process. If you catch yourself holding your breath, just release and let the breath flow naturally again.

Centering – Focus awareness in the part of your body that usually feels off when you are disturbed by something.

Scanning – Survey all the areas of your life that have some problematic issues and make a list of possible subjects to work with.

Selecting – Determine which area of your life is really causing you the most difficulty. Rather than starting with whatever emotion is on the surface at the time of the session, you let the body indicate what it thinks is the root of the problem and start there.

Experiencing – Give it your full attention and allow yourself to really feel all of it. Note how intense a feeling it is on a scale of 0-10.

Visualizing – Develop a clear image representing the feeling.

Naming – Clarify what sort of stuck energy it is you are dealing with.

Appreciating – Understand that the feeling is trying to help you get love, safety or freedom, however primitive its methods may be, and send it love in return.

Receiving – Allow yourself to watch whatever comes up without judgment. Remember to keep breathing freely.

Acting – Evaluate the level of remaining emotional charge and if necessary use energy healing modalities to release any blocked physical energy that is still holding part of the emotion.

Savoring – Savor your new sense of spaciousness now that the clouding emotion is gone.

The Details

Let's look at each of these 12 steps in more detail. As you read, alternate between thinking about what is being described and actually doing each step. If you just read through this chapter you will not come back to it, you will not learn the method, and you will not reap the benefits of emotional mastery that are right at your fingertips now.

Let your first read be your first practice. Once you see the benefits it will be easier to discipline yourself to use the method when you face emotional turmoil in life and need a tool you can use to cut through. Then you can find the inner guidance you need to handle the problem situations of your life when you need it most instead of having to wait until the emotional "noise" dies down enough for you to hear your inner voice.

The method will take you about 30 minutes to do this time, because you are also reading. In practice it only takes about 15-20 minutes once you know what steps to take and are just doing it. Time-wise, that is pretty cheap compared to the hours you normally lie awake with your mind running around the same problem over and over again. Instead of brooding for hours, you could be learning and releasing in minutes.

Grounding

Close your eyes and draw your attention inward with the intention that you are going to learn and heal through this process. Take a minute to feel your feet on the ground or in some other way deepen your awareness of your connection to the Earth.

Breathing

Become aware of your breath moving in and out. Don't try to breathe deeply, as that will cause you to hyperventilate. Just let the breath roll in and out at its own pace and notice how it makes you feel depending on how full/shallow, quick/slow, choppy/smooth it is. Keep the energy moving by maintaining some attention on the breath throughout the process. If you catch yourself holding your breath, just release and let the breath flow naturally again.

Centering

Focus awareness in the part of your body that usually feels off when you are disturbed by something. If you aren't sure where that is, recall the first exercise we did in which you generated the feeling of different emotions within yourself. What part of your body did you feel most of those emotions in? Most people will find that it is somewhere in the belly or chest, but it could be anywhere in the body.

Scanning

Survey all the areas of your life that have difficulties, conflicts or confusion and make a list of possible subjects to work with. Common list items are: There's something going on with my car. There's this thing at work. There are issues in this relationship. And so on.

Do not go into each issue now. Just make a list, similar to if you were making a shopping list. If you were intending to buy light bulbs, you wouldn't write on your shopping list whether it would be Sylvania or GE, 40 watts or 60 watts, a pack of 4 bulbs or 6 bulbs – you would just write "light bulbs" then move on to the next item on your shopping list. In this same way, make a list of areas in your life that have been taking some of your mental and emotional energy these days.

Selecting

While staying focused in the part of your body you identified as holding your emotional body's wisdom, slowly go down the list of issue areas you made in the "Scanning" step. As you think about each issue, watch to see how that part of the body responds. Don't try to label the response with words or any concepts. Just feel it.

Go back and forth between the feeling that arises when you begin to think about each issue and thoughts about the issue. Throughout this process, we are after awareness of the feeling, but you use the thoughts to strengthen the feeling whenever it dims and becomes murky. If you start getting lost in thoughts about the problem, just drop the thinking altogether and immerse yourself fully in the feeling. Once you have a felt sense of each item on your list, choose the one that had the strongest response in the body, even if your mind doesn't think it is the most important issue in your life right now.

Experiencing

Now that you have selected the issue to use as a pathway into the depths of your emotional energy system, begin to focus on the issue with full attention until the feelings associated with it are strong. Once the feeling arises, immerse yourself in it fully and allow yourself to really feel all of it. Note how intense a feeling it is on a scale of 0-10.

Remember that we are using the thoughts to generate the feeling, but that the feeling is what we are after. Be skillful in using the thoughts without getting lost inside them.

Visualizing

Begin to question the feeling. If this feeling was a color, what color would it be? If it was a shape, what shape would it be? What size, thickness, density, etc.? Try to get as clear a picture of it as you can. Ask – then wait to see what first response arises from within you.

This feeling wants to be known; that's why it is persisting. It will cooperate with you in your search for understanding. You are developing an effective communication system between its way of communicating and your conscious mind's way of making meaning out of what it perceives. Visual symbols are one meaning system your brain already understands.

Naming

What quality word or phrase would you use to describe this feeling? What word first comes to mind when you ask it, "What is your name?" Words and phrases like, heavy, sadness, anxiety, tight, sticky or "falling into nothingness," are what we are after. Don't edit yourself. Speak directly to the feeling and call it by the first name that arises and see how it responds. Does it feel 100% like, "Yes, that's my name," or is it more like, "Well, that's part of my quality, but it's not my full name?" Keep asking it for its name until you get a 100%, "Yes, that's me," from the feeling.

Appreciating

Understand that the feeling is trying to help you get love, safety or freedom, however primitive its methods may be, and send it love in return. Being able to see that it has value doesn't mean you have to decide you want it to remain just as it is. It will release more easily if you have a relationship of affection with it than if you are in resistance.

Receiving

Hopefully you have been remembering to keep your breath flowing freely throughout this process. If not, at least make sure you are breathing freely now. Now that you have its name and an image of it, sit with the feeling and learn. Watch it. Listen to it. Feel it fully. It will change on its own just by your baring silent witness.

It has been seeking your full attention all this time and now it has it. It will take advantage of the opportunity to let you know what's on its mind. Be ready for flashes of insight about patterns from your childhood or current relationships. Greet whatever comes without judgment or fear. You can handle this. You are perfectly safe. Keep breathing and asking yourself: "What am I feeling now? What is happening within me now? What is it about this situation that makes it so (add whatever word or phrase you got in the 'Naming' step)?"

This step generally takes about as much time as all the other steps combined. It is the heart of the method. Engage in honest dialog with the feeling – seeing it, calling it by its name, asking it questions you sincerely have about who and what it is and what it is trying to tell you. Ask, then listen deeply.

Acting

Rate your current experience of the original conflicted emotion on a scale of 0-10. Most emotional messages will be fully delivered and released within the preceding "Receiving" step. About 5% of the time there is such a strong energetic pattern of the emotion being held in the physical energy system that the energy won't release even after the emotion that was causing it does.

If you get a 0, skip this step and go to "Savoring." If you get a score above 2, repeat the process, since you have likely touched a deeper emotion that is also ready to be cleared today. If you get a score between 1-2, a few simple meridian therapy methods will allow you to clear all emotional residue from your energy system. Maintain <u>full focus</u> on whatever residual tension is left while adding this one minute finishing routine:

1. Using your right hand, brush along the outside back of your left ear, down over your shoulder, all the way down your arm and off your ring finger, exhaling as you release. Repeat up to 3 times if needed. (1-3 seconds)

2. Tap your neck/stomach neurovascular points on the side of your lower jaw. (5-10 seconds)

3. Tap on your triple warmer acupuncture point (the back of your hand between the knuckles of your pinky and ring finger) while allowing your eyes to travel from far left to far right without moving your head. (6 seconds)

4. Now empty your mind of all thoughts and finish by holding the middle finger of one hand in the belly button and the other at your 3rd eye and pulling up gently on both spots. Hold for 12 seconds while breathing in and out deeply, then release.

Savoring

Savor your new sense of spaciousness now that the clouds of emotion have cleared. You will likely feel a sense of lightness, freedom, joy, and peaceful well-being. Many people giggle during this step. Allow yourself to express whatever comes up for you. You are a free being. You are Spirit. Take this time to fully enjoy the experience of feeling like your true self.

***

By using the combination of these cognitive and somatic methods to relate to emotions, you will get full use out of your emotional energy system. Emotions will no longer be chains of confinement. They will instead be teachers, friends, and tools you can use to empower your most joyful visions for creation.

The emotions that don't serve any useful purpose, and may even be poisoning your life, you will immediately let go. The ones that hold precious nourishment you will fully digest. You will become the master of your emotional tool, as it was meant to be, and most importantly, you will be able to hear your inner guidance even in the midst of the most challenging life situations

11 SPIRIT

As she looked into my eyes I felt as if electric currents were running through my veins and time seemed to warp. "Would you like to receive a channeling session?" she asked.

She was Taylor Sand and we were standing in a new age crystal shop in Mendocino, CA. The shop belonged to a friend of hers who was trying to help Taylor go public with her spiritual work by allowing her to offer sessions out of her store. As my mind floated between feelings of excitement, repulsion, longing, and fear, the shop owner came up to encourage me to give it a try.

I really was very afraid, but I was on a spiritual journey, a road trip with my friend Esete to celebrate her 35th birthday, and it felt like it was my turn to receive a special gift from the trip. So I said yes. The reading turned out to facilitate a shift into not only a new phase in my emotional life, but also into a new way of relating to spirit through my work.

At the time I was in my Master's program in Counseling Psychology at a holistic school in San Francisco and had just begun a two year internship program for budding psychotherapists at a highly selective private practice in Berkeley. A week later I had quit the training program, announcing myself a spiritualist not a therapist, and was trying to figure out how I was going to drag myself through the last year of my degree program when I already knew I didn't want to be a psychotherapist. It was still important to me to finish what I had started, but within myself I knew that the shifts I wanted to create within people would happen in one to six sessions (not 2 - 8 years) and would focus on spiritual growth first and foremost.

Fortunately, I didn't really have to choose. I managed to get through the rest of my MA program and to develop my spiritual healing skills more fully. I was already doing energy work at the local AIDS services agency during the last 4 months of my degree program and decided to go further with that instead of doing the supervised counseling hours I would need to become a licensed counselor in the state of California. Over the two years that followed I continued to receive channeled guidance from Taylor Sand, now by phone, and her guides continued to encourage me to develop my own channeling abilities into solid skills.

Finally in 1998 Taylor told me to buy a book called Opening to Channel by Sanaya Roman and Duane Packer. It took me a week to read the book and a year to master its contents. Opening as a channel is a process of spiritual growth, more than the learning of a skill per se. You don't do channeling; you become a clear, open channel.

Channeling eventually replaced energy work as the primary focus of my healing work. I have come to see that the spiritual journey of humanity is at the step where each person needs to be living as his or her higher self at all times. We need to all wake up to who we truly are and create a world that reflects that authentic being with all its natural joy, harmony, and peace.

My spiritual channeling work focuses on helping clients rediscover their true inner essence as Spirit living through a body. For some clients I do this through Learn to Channel classes, but for most it is an individual process. We begin with a Spiritual Expansion session in which I rebalance their energy-field around their central chakra, raise their energetic vibration, connect their energy system with that of their higher self, and work with their higher self to bring through healing energies and guidance from their spiritual guides. At the end of this chapter I am going to share with you some of the guidance I have heard being given to people.

Among the spiritual healing therapies I use there is one approach aimed at helping the client become a direct channel for their own inner wisdom. There are usually four sessions given within a 1-6 week period (preferably over a 4 week period) to get people to this point. The first session is the Spiritual Expansion session described above. Subsequent sessions focus on continuing the spiritual expansion process and anchoring it within every corner of the client's life.

In the last session I lead them in a graduated process of shared channeling that shifts more and more of the channeling from me to them so that ultimately they are channeling for themselves and I am merely helping them to clarify what is coming from Spirit and what is being distorted by their minds. I truly do want to live in a world in which every person is able to channel for themselves and receive a steady stream of guiding wisdom from their higher selves until the division between "higher self" and "self" dissolves and we are all simply being our true selves at all times.

In the Emotion chapter you were already taught two of the emotional processing techniques I teach clients. The most difficulty people have channeling comes from stumbling across disturbing emotions and so cutting off awareness of their inner experience to stop the feelings. Of course, if you can't be aware of communication coming from your own body, which you've lived with all your life, it's going to be even harder to be aware of communication coming from a guide you've just met.

Being able to be fully present with your inner experience is a critical aspect of being able to channel. Furthermore, the mark of a good channel is that he or she doesn't distort the information coming through to please the intellect nor block the information to avoid feeling emotions. So it is important both to be able to clear conflicted emotions so that channeling can happen and to be able to withstand new emotions that may arise in response to the information that is coming in after channeling has begun. Please keep working on the emotional techniques from the previous chapter as you develop your channeling abilities and you will see results flow much more easily.

Unfortunately I can't really teach the energetic techniques I use in the rest of my work within this format, but I want to encourage you to look into therapies you can receive near you that will work with your meridians, axiatonal lines, DNA activation, Reiki energy-field harmonizing, Johrei, and other energy healing modalities. Whether combined or done through separate practitioners, any of these treatments will help you develop yourself as a spiritual channel (and develop other latent abilities) as they open you to an experience of energies that have been flowing around you all your life, just outside your field of perception.

A big part of being a good channel is being a good translator. Your higher self, as well as an angel or spirit guide, communicates with vibrations. In our sensory world vibrations are perceived as sound and color, but there is a much broader array of vibrational stimuli being sent from the realm of spirit. The task of the channel is not only to be open enough to perceive the various stimuli coming through him/her, but to be skilled enough to convert it into some kind of symbolic form that has meaning to humans – words, images, sensations, movement, etc. The energetic techniques mentioned above all help develop the channel's ability to perceive a wider variety of stimuli and translate it into something meaningful.

I also recommend you look at the Opening to Channel book Taylor and I used to help us develop and the book Spiritual Growth (by the same authors) for a more in-depth look at the subject than can be covered in one chapter. This chapter is meant to be a beginning for you, as my meeting with Taylor was a catalyst for me. The journey before you is a grand and glorious one, and I am happy to be some small part of that process for you.

Learning to Channel

Imagine a world in which every person was intimately connected with their highest inner guidance at all times. Not only would such people live beyond the control of anything outside themselves, but they would also be free of the tyranny of social conditioning that has shaped their personalities and minds. They would be beyond habit, responding to life from the depths of their spiritual essence. Would you like to live in such a world? Would you like to be such a person? Channeling one's higher self is the method we can all use to create such a world, one person at a time.

Channeling isn't about connecting with outside entities, such as angels or spirit guides. It can be used for this purpose, but it doesn't have to be. Channeling happens whenever you open your awareness to a consciousness that is not your personality identity and allow information, feelings, or energies to come through. Channeling is more about the process of opening to receive than it is about the object that is perceived.

The process of opening to receive a broader field of data is a gradual one that need never end. We can view the entire path of our lives as that of learning how to be more receptive to life with all its diversity, fluidity and beauty. Learning how to embrace more of existence is really about learning how to love ourselves unconditionally, since our relationships to our "outer" world are merely reflections of our self-relationship.

Much more will be said about this in the final chapter on Relationship, but it is useful to note that the process of opening as a channel will affect more areas of your life than simply allowing you to hear voices. You will be opening up in a variety of ways and creating a life that reflects that ease, grace, and expansive quality. Your life will become more and more full of love as you learn to live from a place of receptivity. Receptivity is the essence of love itself. It is also the most important skill for a channel, since not much is going to happen if you can't receive the information in the first place.

What do you already know about your ability to be loving and receptive? Have you ever noticed that you are more receptive and more affectionate when you are relaxed? Most people sigh and release contracted muscles as a smile spreads across their faces whenever they are filled with a wave of loving emotion. Try acting that out right now and see if the very imitation of the behavior doesn't arouse a warm feeling in you. That's how conditioned you are to relate love and relaxation with one another.

Love and relaxation are related within channeling also. Your higher self is completely attuned to the energy of love. In fact, love is the core note of its energetic vibration. When you relax you become more aligned with the loving energy of your higher self and so it becomes easier to harmonize your energies so that vibrations can flow between you. Relaxing into the loving qualities of your being is therefore an indispensable element of the channeling process.

What conditions make it easiest for you to relax? Does a sense of safety affect how relaxed you are? Trust, optimism, and mental focus are all related to a sense of safety and all affect your ability to open and relax so that channeling can happen. You must trust your ability to control what comes through you, knowing you can stop anytime you want and will not be taken over by outside forces. In fact, not only do you not have to make contact with negative forces, you don't even have to connect with outside entities at all in order to channel – not even guides. In this chapter we will only look at channeling your higher self.

Optimism is also closely linked to a sense of safety. You expect the best. When you think about channeling you should focus on the positive experiences you will have while doing it and as a result of having done it. Instead of worrying about the worst possible outcome, think of the joy, love, peacefulness, and vitality you will feel as your energetic vibration rises to match that of your higher self.

Think of all the wonderful people and events your newly charged energy-field will then attract into your life. Everywhere you go people around you will feel the harmonious, loving quality of your higher self's energy vibration radiating from you. They will be attracted to that beauty and feel more open, generous, and affectionate towards you. Expect the best as you begin to channel and you will find that helps you to open to the experience more easily.

Mental clarity is the other important aspect of channeling that relates to a sense of safety. If your mind is scattered it is probably due to a combination of habit and anxiety. The habit part can only be overcome through disciplined concentration practice. You must build a habit of being able to control your mind so that you can stay focused on the task at hand, channeling, long enough to make contact with your higher self. The anxiety part is another matter. If you are nervous your mind will be jumpy and so will your body, and there is no amount of discipline that will allow you to channel.

If your life is chaotic and you are under a heavy cloud of fear or despair, that is not the time to learn how to channel. It may be the time you most wish you could channel, because you desire guidance on how to improve your situation and the emotional boost of contact with the higher energy vibration of your higher self. But it isn't the time for you to do it.

Focus instead on getting the situations of your life under control and creating a degree of calm within and around you. Get a channeled spiritual guidance session from someone else if you really need direction from on high right away. I received sessions from Taylor for years while my own channeling abilities opened up. Even now when I am in a crisis situation I find myself temporarily unable to perceive my inner guidance clearly.

The first thing I do is a Release Breath session. If I still can't clearly see what I need to do in the situation I will usually call a friend and have them help me through the process. Their loving presence makes me feel more safe and that makes it easier for me to open my channel again. That is one of the reasons channeling classes are so helpful. There is a tremendous reassurance provided by the presence of others within a group that is learning together.

You are ready to open your channel and meet your higher self right now if: 1) You are feeling good right now; 2) When you think about channeling you feel excited, optimistic, and confident of your ability to control the experience at all times; and 3) You are able to focus your attention for at least 5 minutes without getting lost in thoughts about things going on in your life.

If you aren't able to relax and focus, you won't be able to channel. You may "hear" something, but it will be your intellect doing the speaking not your higher self. If that is your situation, just wait. Be patient. You can do this whenever you are ready. When the time is right your channeling will flow with joy and ease.

Preliminary Exercises

Once you have made the connection with your higher self you can either use the time you spend together to relate without words or you can gather information. At the level of being that precedes the symbolic realm of words, healing energies are transferred from areas of greater harmony to those of lesser harmony. Your higher self's energy spontaneously heals and harmonizes your energy-field whenever you are in contact with it.

If you are going to gather information, you will want to prepare your questions ahead of time and have something available to record the conversation. I did automatic writing (writing down the conversations) for years before I began using a tape recorder and speaking. It is good to do a few practice exercises opening up your throat chakra if you intend to do spoken channeling.

Simple exercises such as toning, singing, or chanting can be incredibly useful. Try holding different types of objects in your hand and seeing what sounds want to come out. Play with the idea of translating physical sensations into sounds. Try it with different foods as well. Notice if there is a different type of sound that comes out with fresh vegetables than with grains or canned foods, for example.

After sounds, start playing with colors. Working with a selection of instrumental music, play a few seconds of one song after another and speak the first color that comes to your mind as you listen. You aren't trying to accurately name the color that "should" go with the sounds you are hearing, just to express the vibration you feel from it. You can't be wrong. Remember, your aim is to develop your translation abilities, which requires skill at both sensing and expressing.

Meeting Your Higher Self

What you need: If you have a tape recorder, record yourself reading the upcoming italicized section at a relaxed pace. Speak clearly and pause occasionally so you will have time to formulate a clear image of each step in the process as you listen to the tape later. If you don't have a tape recorder and don't want to buy one, trade off with a friend – you reading the guided journey for them, then they reciprocating for you. As an added bonus you will be able to share the experience with someone you love and continue practicing together as your channeling develops.

There are many different methods channeling teachers use to connect students with their guides or higher selves. There isn't one right way. The point is to use the imaginative power of the human mind to unlock the doors of perception. At first it will feel like you are just imagining whatever is happening. That is fine. Imagination is the closest thing we have to the Spirit realm of instant thought manifestation.

Here things manifest more slowly because we have poorly disciplined minds. We need to be protected from ourselves a bit. But in the Spirit realm what is imagined and what is real have no delay between them. Even in this realm, scientists have conclusively determined that our minds cannot tell any difference between imagined experiences and real ones.

It may take longer for your thought to manifest in the physical situations of your life, but it takes no time for it to manifest as a lived experience to your mind. The same goes for your emotional experience. So then, from the point of view of mind and emotion, it makes no difference whether you are imagining connecting with your higher self or really going off into some new dimension of reality. You will experience the emotional and mental effects of having done so either way!

That said, let us now take a journey of discovery. It is time to meet that aspect of yourself that was never born and will never die, that wise guide within you that has always been whole and healthy, that which loves you and embraces your life completely. It is time to connect with your higher self.

Begin recording/reading aloud:

1. Find a quiet place where you will not be disturbed and sit with your back straight and feet flat on the floor. Alternately, you can sit cross-legged on a cushion on the floor. Have your back supported so you can relax your muscles and maintain some sort of contact with the floor so that your energy is grounded. Keep the back straight to free up the flow of energy along your spinal energy pathways.

2. Close your eyes and become aware of your breath moving in and out. Watch the breath without trying to control it. Awareness is enough. If you notice yourself breathing rapidly or holding your breath, just intend that you will relax and allow the breath to flow naturally.

3. Once you feel a sense of relaxation, focus your attention at the top of your head and imagine that there was a funnel of light there. The funnel is maybe 2-3 inches across where it touches your scalp, but up to 3 feet across at the top of the funnel. This funnel is always there, gently spinning and bringing in a steady stream of pure light energy.

4. Expand your awareness so that you become aware of all three points at the same time: your contact with the floor through your feet or seating cushion, your breath moving in and out, and the funnel of light at the top of your head.

5. Now silently say a prayer and call the energy of the Consciousness of Light to you. You may think of it as Divine energy, Love, life force energy – whatever represents the highest energy of pure goodness to you – but represent it with an image of clear white light.

6. Imagine that your call is answered by a torrent of Consciousness of Light flowing down from above. As it flows down, the funnel at the top of your head easily expands to allow more energy through at once. This flood of light washes through you then radiates outward in all directions at once, cleansing every cell of your body and every layer of your energy-field and filling you with light.

7. You are now sitting immersed in a field of pure light. You are fully permeated by it. The light makes you feel relaxed, clear, and vibrant. Take a moment to enjoy this feeling.

8. Now you are ready to meet your higher self. Anticipate the joy the meeting will bring you and the way it will accelerate your spiritual growth. This is a turning point in your life. Get clear within yourself now as to whether you are fully ready to make the connection and allow your life to change. Ask yourself if you are ready and listen to hear an answer. Only if you get a yes, proceed.

9. Become aware now of the funnel of light at the top of your head and the wide stream of light entering it from above. See the entire pathway of light and imagine that along the path there were steps leading from your body to the realms of infinite light above.

10. At a comfortable, steady pace, begin to walk up these stairs. With each step imagine that you let go of a bit more of your everyday way of thinking and perceiving and become more open to new experiences. Allow your enthusiasm and willingness to grow as you climb.

11. When you reach the top step, imagine that you see a being in the distance. At first the being may not be that clearly defined. Even if you can't see the being clearly yet, you can clearly feel its love for you. Feel your heart opening as you allow yourself to acknowledge and receive this tremendous love the being feels towards you.

12. Invite the being to come closer. As it approaches, feel the energy of its love intensify and your own vibration begin to lift and expand. There may be a feeling of being full of energy and joyful. If tears want to flow, let them. It is just a release of pent up emotion and will support the process.

13. The appearance of the being will become more and more clear as it gets closer, but it may or may not take on a human form. Its body is pure energy, but it may appear in some form that is familiar to you to strengthen the connection between you. The being is your higher self, an aspect of you that is fully connected with the wisdom that is free of all time.

14. When you feel comfortable, invite your higher self to merge with you completely. Feel it coming into your being as you breathe in and out, opening and releasing, opening and releasing, merging and breathing, one at last, one at last, whole again at last.

15. If tears want to flow let them. Continue to breathe and allow the merger to deepen. Once you feel fully connected with your Total Self, rest a moment to savor the experience before continuing....

16. Now ask your higher self any question that seems important to get an answer to right now. Pay attention to whatever sights, sounds, feelings, or intuitions come through after the question is asked. You are learning to communicate in the language of your higher self. It may experiment with different methods of communicating with you, alternately sending you feelings of pleasure or discomfort to signal when you are receiving its message clearly or distorting it. [If recording, pause an adequate amount of time for guidance to be received.]

17. Now that you have made the connection, you can easily come back into communion with your higher self whenever you want. Ask your higher self if there is anything it wants you to do in the coming week to strengthen your ability to connect with it. Once you have the answer, thank your higher self for its loving presence and guidance and say goodbye.

18. Feel your higher self's joy at having made the connection with you and its gratitude for your willingness to receive its love and guidance. Hear it say goodbye then watch as its energy moves away from yours, leaving a fragment of itself within your energy body.

19. Now walk back down the stairs along the pathway of light and re-enter your physical body completely. Allow the stairway to fade out of this dimension. Feel your contact with the ground and focus your attention on your breath moving in and out.

20. Congratulate yourself for what you have just done and rejoice. You have now connected with your higher self and begun a relationship that will change your life forever. When you are ready, open your eyes and come back into the room. You are now an open channel for pure light!

Embodying the Higher Self Within Daily Life

Now that you have established a connection with your higher self you can look to it for guidance whenever you need. I suggest you do seated sessions of connecting with your "Self" on a regular basis. Not only will this provide you with a steady source of useful information, but it will greatly expand your ability to make the connection easily.

Prepare a set of questions for your guide in advance of each session. Good questions to start with include: "What are my lessons in this lifetime? What is the most important thing for me to learn right now? What is my purpose in this relationship (thinking of someone in your life)?" These are all personal questions and are the ones best answered by your higher self, as opposed to universal spirit guides or angels.

I suggest you do the seated sessions with a tape recorder or notebook. Either speak or write each question and the answer to it. Other times you may not want to focus your time with your higher self on gaining information. It may be the energetic rejuvenation and emotional fulfillment of the connection that you seek. Then you will simply sit with your higher self for a period of time then rise refreshed and ready to go through your day feeling more like your true self.

Remember that repetition builds habits. You want to repeat the act of moving into connection with your higher self frequently. That way when you are in the midst of daily life and need inspiration on the fly you can quickly "link up" and get the help you seek.

Though each of you reading this will have gone through the same process in making the initial connection with your higher self, you will each develop your own way of re-establishing the connection over time. Some of you may find that watching the breath and announcing the intention to connect with your higher self is the primary method that works for you. Others will visualize a story unfolding, as we did in the guided meditation you just completed. I tend to focus my attention on my heart or 3rd eye most of the time, though sometimes just announcing my intention to become aware of the presence of my higher self within me is all it takes.

You are always united with your higher self. In the visualization we represented this concept with the fact that some of your higher self's energy was left in your energy body after you parted, but even before the "connection" was ever made your higher self was one with you. Opening as a channel for your higher self isn't about becoming your higher self. You already are your higher self. What you are doing is becoming aware of who you are. This is a gradual process. Little by little you get more comfortable with being who you really are and less attached to being who you have been programmed to pretend to be.

As you move through each day, try to do two things as much as you can. Connect with your higher self frequently, even just to check in and say, "Are you still there?" and watch for a response of some kind within you. Also, gradually lengthen the amount of time you spend with your higher self each time you connect.

Ultimately the idea is to move beyond the idea of "it and you" and simply be your higher self. Then when you think of "me" the me will be your higher self speaking.

Why do this? Remember joy. Remember love. Remember immortality and wisdom. Remember peace and ease and harmony and creating a habit of surrendering to the experience of being all of that, so that you never again need to pursue any of it outside yourself. Remember the promise of wholeness and be it. Is that reason enough?

Spiritual Practices

At the end of a Spiritual Expansion session the higher self or spirit guides of the client almost always give the person instruction in practices the client can do after the session to further accelerate their spiritual growth. Many times as I hear these messages coming through me I think to myself, "That sounds like something it would be good for me to do too. I'm going to try that sometime." And I do. And it is. Here is a sampling of practices for you to try.

If you are a heart centered person, you will advance along your spiritual path most easily by engaging the presence of Spirit in your life using your heart. Loving touch is the most concrete expression of heart energy. Try touching the objects you use throughout the day as if they were precious loved ones. Feel the sensation of lovingness in your very fingertips as you caress the object.

A good opportunity is when you are washing the dishes. Wash each item as if you were bathing a beloved child – or if you are the sensuous type, a lover. Touch everything with love and you will feel your heart opening to embrace the Divine within all things. Out of this, your eyes will also open to see the Divine within all things. All your senses will expand to perceive the world as beloved.

If you are stimulated by color and shape, buy a drawing book to use as a Sacred Arts journal. Get out your favorite art supplies (colored pencils, pastels, etc.) and open to the second page of the book so that you have two sheets facing up at once. Using the techniques presented earlier in this chapter, open the connection with your higher self so that you can channel. Once the connection is established, begin to draw whatever flows from your inner inspiration on the left side page. Do not edit yourself or try to figure out what is being drawn. Just flow with it. After you are done, meditate on your drawing for a few minutes. Then write whatever emerges on the right side page. Use your journal as often as possible and at the end of each month review everything you have put in it so far.

If your childhood memories of feeling peaceful and fully connected to life involve time spent in nature, make a practice of strengthening your relationship with the Earth. This planet is not an object any more than you are just because you have a body. It is alive. It is a fully conscious living being, just like you. In fact, it is an enlightened master! As often as you are able, go out into the woods or down to the sea and find some aspect of nature that you can relate to as a living being relating to another living being.

Hug a tree and feel it hugging you back. Play with the ocean. Tease it and see how it reacts. (Just be ready to run fast!) Talk to the wind and watch what happens. Think of each meal you eat as a dish prepared by Mother Earth and sent to you with love. Move into intimate personal relationship with the life that is pulsing all around you and you will discover deeper layers of what it means to be Spirit living in a human body on the planet called Earth.

Go someplace you will not bother anyone and fully release the power of your voice. Sing, yell, scream, laugh, whatever wants to come, let it. Sing it out then listen to hear it echo back to you. Even if there is no acoustic echo, there will be a lasting reverberation in the objects around you. If you are open, attentive, and receptive you will hear the echo of your sound within the silence that follows it. Continue the process of alternating "sounding" and listening until the sound of even your screams becomes music to your ears.

All of these practices open your energy flow so that you can either express or perceive more fully. Some train you to allow the spontaneous expression of who you are right here and now. Others help you tune in more deeply to the presence of being in the objects around you. The idea is to open more and more fully to an experience of all of you meeting all of life until the boundary between "you" and "all" blurs into nothingness.

There is no out in "out there." You are the dish and the tree and the sea and the sound of your voice echoing in the silence. You are all things everywhere and have been for all of time. You believe. Now it is time for you to know. I hope this helps.

12 RELATIONSHIP

Whether we call it the luminous emptiness, the "Ultimate All," Spirit, the Goddess, God or something else, we can ascribe a few basic characteristics to the ultimate level of reality the human mind can conceive. It is infinite in Its ability to appear in any form, but It has no one form in which It is permanently held that could be called Its true form.

Though we cannot really ascribe much to It in the way of intrinsic qualities It possesses, we can say that when It is encountered by the human mind It is perceived as an experience of joy, peace, love, and harmony. Moreover, It appears to possess one essential quality that could be thought of as a personality characteristic. That is self-love.

The All-Pervading Light, the Ultimate All, God – loves Itself completely.

This understanding of God is essential for our developing a proper understanding of right relationship. If we are in fact Spirit relating to Spirit, this self-love should show in all our interactions. When we are fully embodying our true Spirit selves, this is how we will relate to all we meet. There will be a spontaneous flow of healing compassion from that which is whole to that which is wounded whenever an imbalance exists between two energies and both are open to relating.

There was a time once when my compassion was so strong that I could heal people just by looking at them. I recall the first time I noticed I had the ability. I was sitting in a café in Oakland, CA waiting for the café staff to make me a fish taco. I decided to pass the time watching people walk down the street outside the café's huge windows.

At the time I wasn't feeling much inside myself. I felt oddly numb actually. There was a feeling of peace and a buzzing feeling of bliss within my body, but it was more like a blanket feeling (that had no variation no matter what was happening) than an emotion (which is generally a response to some type of stimulus). I was completely non-reactive. It was as if the world was a hazy, very far away place and yet fully inside me at the same time.

I wasn't accustomed to that energy state of utter peace within my emotions. I could still feel emotions arising in my emotional body, but there was nothing arising out of me. All I could feel in my emotional body were other people's emotions!

I felt starved for emotional drama. Even the "feeling" of their emotions wasn't really a feeling. As each person walked past the café's windows I got a general impression of their emotional state that my mind would spontaneously label with names like sadness, fear, or withdrawal. However, this was all happening between my newly super-perceptive emotional body and my keen mental body, which had no confusion as to where the emotions were being generated. Meanwhile, I was actually identified within my spiritual body, which was feeling no variations, just an infinite field of peace.

I was in complete security, abundance, and self-love. I was also in complete compassion, so firmly knowing my oneness with all beings that I could experience all that was within them as if it was within me. But there was nothing actually within me. And peace, abundance, self-love and the lot aren't as exciting as you think when there is no contrast. It is relief from suffering that feels like pleasure. When we simply are everything, there is curiosity and interest, but no emotional variation. It was dull, dull, dull.

Oh my goodness. I have offended some of you. I just said that "enlightenment" was dull. Well it was actually what is called a satori experience, not enlightenment, which is a more stable achievement. Of course, it was dull to me because I wasn't really ready for it. I was given the chance to taste it, but my still active ego wanted excitement more. I longed for the cycles of ups and downs in response to changes outside myself which constituted the feeling of being alive to me. I also did not have the structures set up in my life to give me opportunities to relate to people Spirit to Spirit, as I longed to do while I was in that state.

It's a shame I wasn't ready to stabilize in that expansive state, because I had amazing powers not only to compassionately feel what others were feeling during that time, but as I mentioned earlier, I could heal people with a glance! I think I was able to do it (or rather that it was spontaneously happening, since I wasn't actively doing anything per se) as a natural effect of fully embodying one's higher self. Recall from the fourth chapter on Conviction the effects of Ultimate Bodhicitta. I had taken a first step along that path, however temporarily.

As each person walked past the café I could perceive their emotional state and the wholeness of my higher self at the same time. I could also perceive that wholeness within me as if it was within them. That "only one of us" thing goes both ways. I could feel them within me and me within them.

The darkness within their energy bodies and the light shining through me could not exist simultaneously within their energy field. So the clear light obliterated the darkness. It happened instantly. I had just enough time to notice them, perceive whatever their hang up was, and feel my wholeness. Then it was as if the first perception just evaporated.

Suddenly the man who was walking along in a daze, distracted completely by a mind spinning out of control, stopped dead in his tracks and, looking down at himself, realized he was in a body. Imagine that, a body. Hmm. And the woman who was in deep despair suddenly stopped in her tracks, looked blankly in my direction, then proceeded down the street with a gentle smile spreading across her face.

One after another, they walked past and one by one they let it all go. Each one would look in my direction before continuing down the street, but the glare from the late afternoon sun on the glass windows seemed to cause them to see only their own reflections.

Compassion means to experience your oneness with others so clearly that you literally feel with them (com=with, passion=feeling). Within this unified being, healing energy spontaneously flows from areas of harmonious energy into those of disturbed energy, bringing balance and well-being.

I was able to heal people without even thinking about it, but my new boundless perception wasn't restricted to humans. A few weeks after that I was at Golden Gate Park and for the first time in my life I could communicate with trees. By then I had already started to rebel against my new energy state so I was feeling some emotion within me again, but I was still pretty open and still awfully perceptive. I'm glad I was because it was an unforgettable experience.

Did you know that Pine trees are incredibly loving? They are like mothers. Their love is warm and sweet, very intimate. Eucalyptus are emotional purifiers. You can pour out your tears and they will cleanse every corner of your heart. No problem for them at all. I found Oaks to be a little intimidating. I know some people love them, but they weren't my cup of tea.

Not only do different families of trees have distinct family characteristics, but the individual trees also have unique personalities. I noticed this especially among the Pine trees I met. There are as many different kinds of mother's love among the Pines as there are among human mothers. I could have stayed with the Pines forever. I loved feeling their emotions. Unfortunately San Francisco is rather cold at night and eventually I had to go indoors.

Alone I was emotionally flat – just rock-steady peace and well-being with no concept of time passing or anything being accomplished. With humans I was an endless ocean watching waves of other people's misery and relief pass through it with no response within my emotional body. Everything felt thoroughly unreal and fairly irrelevant. Given that I was still identified with my ego, it was not fun.

After a month I managed to reignite my emotional karma and I was back in the game. I was able to identify with my emotions again and once more able to feel the cycles of suffering and relief that I recognized as joy.

I share all of this with you not so that you will say, "You dolt," though I realize that is a distinct possibility. I know. It is absurd to touch upon the experience of enlightenment and decide to run from it. You think that is the height of what human experience adds up to, and it is, in the end. But would you begrudge a 4 year old for wanting to skip rope rather than learn how to add and subtract? Yes, the child must learn, but 6 is soon enough for addition and subtraction. At the time I decided that "someday soon" was perfectly adequate for my fully waking up as well. I needed to progress to that state within every corner of my life so that my life supported that level of expansion.

How 'bout you? Are you ready now? I'm hoping I am. That's why I'm writing this book. It is my offering to you, but you are me. I am waking myself up through writing this for us. I hope that by the time it reaches you I will be fairly stable in my awareness of my true self. I believe I am now ready for the drama to end and I am quite curious to see what that is like over the long haul. If you see me pitching a fit, you can assume I wasn't as ready as I had hoped.

Although I am hoping my natural humor will come out this time. Often during brief periods of oneness with my higher self – hours here and there – I find myself laughing out of the pure joy of being. My laughter touches those around me and fills them with joy too, carrying the vibration deep into their being.

I think that mirthful quality did not show itself during my month-long expansion of consciousness because it was a forward glimpse of what was possible, not the stable achievement of it. (Is it possible to be a depressed enlightened person?) Also, what I really wanted to do during that time was to just sit with people in silence. That's why I liked being with the trees so much. We would just "BE" together, without having to do or say anything. All action was so clearly irrelevant, but the intrinsic beauty of all beings was so delightful, I just wanted to drink that in.

My boredom was at being surrounded by so much artifice all the time. I longed for real interaction, but no one was meeting me at that level. This is yet another example of how we are all connected. Even Heaven can be a lonely place if you have to live there alone.

Healing relationship is one of the most important things we are doing on this planet. When we use ourselves to help others heal, we heal the part of ourselves that is them and we create a world in which we can frolic with delight as a Buddha among Buddhas.

One-to-One

The same rules apply to romance as to any other human relationships.

Here's the bottom line: Stop making things up.

If you are going to be in relationship with anyone, whether the grocer at the corner store or your significant other, you have got to get real. That is exactly why I am so impatient with romance. What people call romance is usually just fantasy. If two people agree to play the same game at the same time it's called a passionate love affair, but if one person's fantasies are unrequited, that is called stalking. Romance is fickle.

That said, sometimes two people who are truly in alignment with one another for a significant phase of their lives happen to meet and the conditions are right for them to form an intimate, ongoing relationship. If they can relate to each other as Spirit loving Spirit, they can have a Divine relationship. That is the highest use of any relationship – be a demonstration of God loving God.

Even if a couple can't go that far, they can still have a relationship that supports mutual spiritual development along a path of joy if both people hold that ideal. Marriage relationships can present the very best learning environments, especially if both people consider learning and growth as something fun to do. If there is resistance to self-reflection and conscious personal responsibility, the relationship will still teach, but it will be teaching along the path of suffering. In healthy relationship the couple gets to grow on a path of joy.

If you meet someone who seems to open your heart, just by their mere presence, that's a good indication that a rewarding relationship might be had with them. This is especially so if you have the same effect upon them. Bringing out the best in one another is an excellent foundation for a relationship.

The essential aspects of healthy relationship are:
- Authenticity;
- Adaptability;
- Self-love;
- Awareness of the equality among both parties;
- Some degree of awareness of their unity, however fleeting;
- The ability to accept the other person just as they are with no hope of having them change in any particular way, but a willingness to seeing them change in whatever way. This is another aspect of not making things up. You don't make up the past, present, or future. You relate to them with acceptance in each now moment and let time take care of the rest.

You don't have to be fully enlightened before you can have healthy relationships. These are not descriptions of enlightened qualities, other than some degree of awareness of unity. Even that is not enlightenment, it is simply a mark of having embarked upon the road towards enlightenment.

The most important item on this list is self-love. If you cannot treat yourself with kindness, patience, and forgiveness you are not going to be able to relate to your partner in a healthy way. In fact, the closer someone gets to you the more you will treat them as an extension of yourself.

If you tend to be hard on yourself, critical, demanding, maybe even self-deprecating, you are going to have to work on that if you don't want to be judgmental, controlling, and demeaning towards your loved ones. Similarly, if you are entering into a relationship with someone who is very self-critical, but who treats you with kindness, be aware that the closer you get to this person the more they will probably start treating you the same way they treat themselves.

Which isn't to say you shouldn't engage with them. The psycho-emotional healing that can happen within relationship is one of the greatest beauties of relationship. So long as you don't try to heal them and so long as they truly want healing for themselves and take responsibility for it themselves, you can make a very positive difference in the world through extending healing relationship to the people you meet.

Within yourself, just hold an understanding of their confusion about their worth along with your certainty about their true Buddha nature and send them loving thoughts. Watch for your own tendencies to judge, and decide to forgive, accept, and embrace them instead. Recall Dr. Emoto's research findings on the ability of loving thoughts to bring health and harmony to bodies of water. Your loving thoughts are powerful.

Helping one another heal is an incredibly important part of human relationship. If you have been working on your channeling this can provide a valuable tool in such a situation. You may be able to tune into your higher self to understand what they need rather than trying to analyze them with your lay-psychiatry. Whatever emerges from your higher self's wisdom will be just the thing to give them the opening they need to shift out of old patterns and open to new experience. Then it is up to them whether they are ready for growth into health. Whatever they decide, don't judge. Accept them as they are.

Love creates the safe space that is needed for people to heal themselves.

Self-Love: The Ultimate Relationship

Self-love can act as a litmus test for when you are in full alignment with your higher self. As a clear reflection of God, the higher self is unwavering in its self-love, just as God is. If you are not feeling loving towards yourself, you are out of alignment. Don't just stay that way. Do something about it.

You will not be able to have healthy relationships with anyone else until you have one with yourself. What we love most in others is usually the way we see ourselves reflected back by them. We love who we are when we are with them, so we love their company. Because we love their company, over time we come to love them. Here I am speaking of real relationships, not romantic fantasies (which tend to be instantaneous misunderstandings rather than experiential closeness that grows over time). All love in life begins with self-love. It is therefore the most important relationship of your life.

So what do you do if you realize you are a person who doesn't really love him/herself? The most accessible approach is to practice forgiveness. You can forgive yourself any time you want. You don't need any special outside conditions or any help from anyone else. This forgiveness is most thorough when you remind yourself that you are making mistakes within a dream world. You seem to be imperfect because you seem to be living in an imperfect world that is real. But it isn't real, and neither are your imperfections.

If this is too much of a stretch for your belief system, then just look at it this way, abusing yourself isn't going to improve the situation. You will still be prone to mistakes in judgment and inadequacies in ability from time to time. If you take a hostile stance towards yourself you will hide much of your problems within your unconscious to try to protect yourself from punishment. That will allow those imperfections to grow. But if you are gentle and accepting towards yourself, that will make it easier to face the deeper aspects of your unconscious so that healing can occur.

A forgiving attitude towards yourself is a crucial aspect of healing and growth. Another important healing relationship it that with others. Humans are social animals, and growing within relationship is hard-wired into our neurological systems. That is why babies fail to thrive if they are not given sufficient loving attention, particularly loving touch.

I know it sounds like a bit of a catch-22 – you have to love yourself before you can have a healthy relationship and you must have a healing relationship before you can love yourself. Actually, it is easier than that, though still not exactly a piece of cake. It is a challenging endeavor that will take all of your focus and commitment if you really want to heal. The important thing is for you to understand that healing is not only possible, but ultimately inevitable. Someday, within some lifetime, each of us will be fully awake and living from a place of complete inner wholeness.

While most relationships need to be mutual in order to last, consisting of two parties with fairly equivalent levels of maturity and health, not all are. In order to have a healthy relationship of equals you need to have some degree of self-love developed already, but long before that you can have healing relationships with those who are more developed than you are.

The most valuable one of these relationships is that with a wise and loving spiritual teacher who is always available at any time of the day or night as soon as you open yourself to receive guidance. That teacher is, of course, your higher self. Spend as much time as you can receiving love and guidance from silent communion with your own spiritual self and you will begin to heal and grow. Its constant love for you will become natural too you as well.

The next best type of healing relationship is that within friendships and professional helping relationships, such as those with teachers, counselors, or mentors. That way there is not a requirement of mutuality. Friendships are best when there is mutuality, of course, but we can comfortably be friends with a wider variety of people than we can join lives with in marriage-type relationships. There is no threat to personal survival or to our core self-concept within the friendship and we know we can create more distance anytime we want by just becoming conveniently "busy" until we have energy for helping our friend-in-need once more. Within Tibetan Buddhism a lama is often referred to as one's spiritual friend.

Professional helping relationships often present the most effective healing environments. Many people consider it a mark of shame to need to pay someone to provide loving attention, but that is a terrible misunderstanding that prevents many people from getting the help they need. The reality is, if you need to receive a lot of anything from someone you had better be prepared to give them a lot of something in return. An imbalance in the flow of energy can only exist for so long before resentment grows and anger or even hatred results.

If both parties had equal emotional health there would be a natural mutuality to the flow of generosity between them. But if one is significantly more healthy than the other, he/she will do most of the giving and the other party will do most of the receiving. In that case, there had better be some other area in which energy is flowing in the opposite direction to balance the relationship. I would argue that it is better to pay someone outright than to have a relationship in which you never stop "paying" for the "love" you are receiving through unreasonable demands for time, money, praise, or whatever your partner decides to extort. That they are more healthy than you while you are not feeling your self-love does not mean they are perfect. There is an unconscious drive to balance the scales and they will try to get something back from you if you aren't giving them an equal amount of emotional support.

Relationships in which one party is significantly more emotionally healthy than the other are best to not be marriage-type relationships.   Otherwise massive conflicts will frequently arise due to the energetic imbalance between them. This will interfere with either partner's ability to stay centered within their wholeness. Instead of the relationship lifting one party up, it will pull both down.

The other benefit of paying up front is that you can shop around for someone who is highly skilled in helping people emotionally heal rather than having to settle for whoever you can find who's willing to play lay-therapist for you. Psychotherapists make good choices for relationships that will help you build self-love. Even among them you should shop around. When I had therapy I interviewed 8 therapists before I settled on the one for me. Fortunately, at the time I was in California, where there are approximately 60,000 licensed psychotherapists.

Spiritual teachers are often great healers also, though not all draw upon spiritual philosophies that honor the importance of self-love. If your teacher comes from the school of "all life on Earth is suffering so stop thinking about your happiness and learn what I am teaching you so you can escape this world once and for all" I doubt you are going to learn much about loving your life or loving yourself unconditionally. One of the things I love so much about my current spiritual teacher is that it appears the only thing he wants in exchange for his loving support is that you use it to awaken as your true self. That's his payoff.

Direct relationship with the realm of Spirit, whether relating to your higher self or to spirit guides, is my preferred healing relationship for everyone. It makes a great supplement to psychotherapy, and no one should be seeing any spiritual teacher without also having a direct relationship with their own inner guidance. Hopefully you are still working on your channeling every day and are seeing that relationship strengthen and grow.

The love that comes from the realm of Spirit is the one perfect relationship we can rely upon in life. Even mothers need a break sometime, but Spirit just keeps on giving, never needing anything in return. The more time you spend in communion with Spirit the more you will get used to feeling the same way about yourself that It feels about you. You will get used to being awash in self-love. Please set aside ample time for developing this relationship. Dwell in communion with your loving higher self for as many hours as you can each day.

Relationship to Place

The most often overlooked relationship in America is that to place. People tend to move through the world as if their feet weren't touching the ground. They visit beautiful Maui, a magical land of healing and renewal, and return home never having noticed anything beyond the same sunshine, blue water, and fabulous entertainment of any resort island. Sure they love it, but what was it they loved? They never actually met the island itself. If you can fully be wherever you are, really be fully present there, you will touch infinity. You will take the inner road into blissful oblivion.

The next time you are on Maui, drive all the way around West Maui, and stop a while by the side of the road. Or go far in the opposite direction, Hana way. Get off the beaten track so that you can have some much needed alone time with your new lover.

As soon as you get some privacy, make love to the land. Gaze lovingly into her horizons and feel her looking back. Bend down and touch her soil. Rub some on your hands. Don't worry about getting dirty. It's loving dirt. It's full of love for you. You will feel the land's loving caress if you are willing to let her touch you and if you pay close attention.

Receptivity to the other is the cornerstone of true love. There must be a willingness to fully take the other in and let them change you. This change does not come about by scheming or manipulating. They have no deliberate intent that you change. In fact, it is because they are so totally accepting towards you that you are able to drop your defenses and allow in the new experiences that will eventually lead to change within you. That is the healing power of love.

Wherever you are, let the land love you. Touch it. Look at it. Talk to it. Give it your attention with an open heart and be ready to experience something new. Be there fully. Breathing in and breathing out, become a little less you and a little more Earth. The willingness to breathe is all that is necessary.

Relationship to Time

Past and future do not exist apart from the perceiver who experiences them. At an ultimate level, there is no such thing as past or future. Memories of the past are actually present moment thoughts. Hopes and fears about the future are really present moment thoughts too. Everything that happens – thought, feeling, action, outside events – is happening right now.

The passage of time is the product of how the human physical system relates to reality. The synapses within our brains take a certain amount of time to fire and so duration is programmed into our perceptive system. With that comes sequence, as this now moment is followed by this now moment is followed by another, and so on.

The combination of duration and sequence is what we experience as time. Even your experience of time is just as fluid as any other relationship. Have you noticed that 10 minutes can either mean rushing out the door 5 minutes late or pacing up and down waiting for someone to arrive, depending on your perspective? To the first person 10 minutes flew by so fast they were 5 minutes short in their experience of it. To the second person 10 minutes drags on and on as if it will never end.

Time is an essential relationship for beings at our level of development because it allows us to learn. By looking at how this present thought or action leads to this later experience, we learn to watch ourselves creating. If it were happening too quickly we would have chaotic lives because our minds are still pretty wild and we are still fairly irresponsible. We need a realm of slow manifestation, so time was programmed into our realm, both within us and within our environment.

Time is important to us in its natural form as a progression of experiences that occur in a linear succession of present moments, but it is also beneficial to catch glimpses of non-sequential reality. These glimpses serve to inspire us and help us leap ahead in our development. It is good to mix linear progression in with leaps ahead, both within the experience of time and within the experience of learning and growth.

Predicting the future is only useful when it is used to shorten our learning curve by showing us possible futures resulting from the choices available to us now instead of our having to live each choice out before we can see where they lead. Leaps backwards to look at the past can also be valuable in that the understanding gained can help us leap ahead in our learning curve just as much as forward glimpses do.

However we relate to time, the most important thing is to not forget that we are in fact relating. It is not a static "reality" so much as a fluid relationship. Only with that understanding is choice possible. As in any relationship, we get to make choices affecting our learning, growth, and joy. What role does time play in your life? Is it a friend or an enemy? Likely it alternates between the two. What if you could fully accept each moment just as it is?

Within healthy relationship this is what we always strive to do, to accept the other party fully just as they are without trying to change them. Only then are they given sufficient space in which they can expand and reveal all the blessings they came into our lives to share. Only then are we receptive enough to receive any of it. Could you relate to this moment with full acceptance? Could you allow yourself to discover the mysteries of its hidden blessings? Would you? When?

Wholeness and Parts in Relationship

Relationship occurs whenever there are parts interacting with one another instead of a existing as a united whole. There is a desire for integration among the parts, but parts can never add up to create a whole. There is a distinct difference between harmony and wholeness. For example, within the context of time, step-by-step progression is normal reality and eternity is the level of wholes. In terms of civilization, as humans we are learning how to relate to one another harmoniously, but as Spirit we are whole.

There are two levels of existence, The Ultimate and reflections of the Ultimate relating to one another. We are obviously in that second level. That is where the learning and growth occurs, the self-discovery. It is as if Spirit was enjoying the process of looking at Itself through each of us. Imagine that Spirit loves watching us relate to one another, especially loving it when It gets to watch Itself expressing Its true love for Itself. What if Spirit is in love with love?

The way I see it, if not for free-will, if Spirit could have Its way, all relationship would just be love loving itself. Time, place, romance, healing – it would all be used to display love flowing out into the world without boundaries.

And this is our destiny. For just as we once seemed to move out from the singular to the plural, the plurality is moving back towards integration and eventually full unity within wholeness. I say "seemed" because none of it really happened within this made up world of ours. That is what we will eventually discover once we awaken to wholeness again, but that is not the next step in our collective development.

In this current lesson, we are heading towards a collective future of harmony, love, and peace. This "Heaven on Earth" is a preliminary experience along the return path to the void of full Unity consciousness, but it is the one worth our attention since there is no point in thinking about our experience of the end of experience. The next level of our development is close at hand and it truly promises the manifestation of perfect relationship within all areas of human experience if enough of us can make the shift into living as our true selves.

We don't have to become something new. We don't have to add or achieve anything. We just have to be willing to breathe in and breathe out. We just have to be willing to say yes to each moment, fully, as it unfolds. Love each moment. Love life. Forgive the imperfections you perceive and say yes to life. Heaven is at the tip of our noses and all it takes is for enough of us to breathe a little more deeply, be a little more willing, and let it in.

This is a glorious time to be alive. There is a shift in consciousness just around the corner. Even the doomsayers are poised to let go of their addiction to negative creation and embrace a destiny of global awakening – though they might not admit it.

We are awash in a tremendous amount of love and light right now. There are light beings coming from every corner of numerous dimensions to assist us in this transition. They are overjoyed at the chance to be a part of this new bud's flowering. There are so many high guides making themselves available that some people have 10 guides! Everyone wants in on the action. Someday they will be able to say they knew us when and look at us now.

You don't believe me? What? Do you see apocalypse? Let's talk a bit about apocalypse.

Relating To Our Destiny

If you hold a vision of an apocalyptic future, that is not a prediction. It is an intent to create. You are declaring that you want "them" to pay for their ignorance, destructiveness, selfishness and greed. In fact, you want them to pay so badly that you are willing to sacrifice all future generations for the satisfaction of seeing them suffer. "That's justice," you say, "That's what they get."

In your rage, you want to see them choking on the toxic fumes from their Hummers, their arteries bursting with fats from their heartless gorging on animal flesh, their children gunned down at school while they support the NRA. You want them to get what they have paid for.

This is not a prediction you are tuning into with your psychic skills or powers of analytical reasoning as you listen to the scientific reports rolling in. That is a cop out. No, this is your wish. You choose this future for this world because you refuse to forgive.

I know there is great resistance in you to accepting this. You want to see yourself as the innocent one who is simply willing to see what is there before your eyes for anyone to see. They are the ones in denial. That's why they are ruining the world for us all. You are a victim, screaming at the top of your lungs for them to stop and trying to live a good example with your life. You are not like them. You are innocent.

You are deluded, as are they. It is your hostility fueling their destructive rage. It is your greed driving them to strip every last ounce of "value" out of the planet that gives itself freely to all who pass through. It is your primal fear that causes them to grasp after every scrap of food they can get their hands on and cram it into their overflowing mouths, killing themselves with excess while millions of people starve.

"How is this?" you protest! Because they are you. There is no separation between us. There is only one of us. THERE IS ONLY ONE OF US.

So long as you maintain insistence that they are doing something to you, or to anyone else, you are invigorating the same system of delusion that causes them to behave the way they do. It is their belief in separation combined with some experience of deprivation, whether in childhood or a previous life, that naturally leads them to behave the way they do. Had you been exposed to the same stimuli you would also react as they are reacting so long as there is confusion about the one basic truth of our existence – there is only one of us.

Forgive them. Be pardoned yourself.

When you are ready to say that you would rather see 1000 guilty men in Heaven than one innocent man in Hell, you are ready to begin the process of helping to create Heaven on Earth. You then become part of the solution. Really there is no Heaven nor Hell and no guilty nor innocent, but the point is that only when you could say that if there were these conditions you would choose as such, only then is there hope for you. Until then you are just like them.

I don't mean to be hard on you, but if you are engaging in negative creation you must take this seriously. You must stop. The more powerful your creative powers become the more dangerous you will be. You must shift into a pattern of positive creation when it comes to what you see in our collective future.

If you can really see all 1001 of these people as aspects of yourself you can take the first step towards true world service. The second step is to be clear about your connection to the unalterable, unwavering, unconditional, pure self-love of your God self. Both result from complete merger with your higher self.

Once I was driving along and saw a young man wearing a t-shirt with a Nazi cross on the back. I was instantly filled with rage and wanted to stick a knife right through that cross and into his back. The violent thought further ignited my anger while simultaneously giving me a sense of satisfaction. Looking more closely into the feeling of rage I saw that its core was my disgust at his cowardly aggression. He was using the shirt to express his hatred towards non-whites, and telling someone you hate them, however indirectly, is an act of violence. But stabbing someone in the back is an act of cowardly aggression too.

I also saw his symbolic act as one of terrorism. He wanted any non-white to see his shirt and, remembering the extensive history of white violence against people of other races, become afraid. But I also wanted all white people to see that knife sticking through that Nazi cross on his back and get the message, "This is what will happen to you if you choose to publicly wear this symbol of hatred." I wanted them to be too afraid to do what he had done even if they sympathized with his racist views.

The more closely I looked at my anger, the more I saw my connection to that young neo-Nazi. I realized that my sense of justice and righteous indignation was really just a cover for the same symbolic aggression the young man was enacting. The only difference was that he was doing it and I was just wishing that I could legally and morally get away with doing it.

As soon as I saw that he and I were basically the same, my natural understanding, acceptance, and forgiveness towards myself immediately extended to include him. I released the anger and felt a brotherhood with that young neo-Nazi that I could never have anticipated. Instead of wishing to see him pay for his offensive choice of attire, I wanted to see him feel safe enough in this world to not need to dominate or terrorize anyone.

In that moment, I recognized our Oneness and with that clarity I saw that there was no one to attack and no one to be attacked. With the veils of illusion stripped away, all that remained was Spirit in its wholeness.

When nothing can shake you from your experience of the love within you, when no dark corner can snuff the light of your self-awareness, when you recognize everything you perceive as an illusory display of your beloved Self – then you are ready to be a world healer.

Then you can forgive everyone everything and walk through the doors of the prison that has locked us all in a needless cycle of famine, war, disease, blame, shame, and despair for hundreds of thousands of years. Then, standing with your feet planted firmly on the ground, you will look up into a clear and spacious sky and sing from the depths of your being:

Free of the past, free of the past, thank God Almighty, we are free of the past.

***

We are like an infinite Light watching reflections of itself interact. We are dreaming a dream of division and diversity. To be a separate part is lonely, painful, and frightening. However much we bury our awareness of that, the feelings themselves will always be there so long as we believe in our separation.

The separation is just a dream. There is only one of us. We are and have always been whole. We are untouchable in our perfection. Wake up and set your reflected aspect free. Heaven is here whenever you have eyes to see it, for when the eye is open, all is light. You are that light and it is time to reveal your true nature – now.

THE END

ABOUT THE AUTHOR

Author Indigo Ocean is the founder of the Phone Buddies emotional support and peer counseling community and former host of the top-rated talk radio show "Together in Spirit" - with guests including Byron Katie, A.H. Almaas, and James Twyman.

In addition to a BA from Brown University, Indigo holds an MA from the CA Institute of Integral Studies in Integral Counseling Psychology, a holistic form of psychotherapy that addresses the spiritual and energetic aspects of psychological health. She is a Reiki Master and Johrei practitioner who has helped hundreds of people transform their lives through intensive 1-hour energy healing sessions.

With a focus on service since her teen years, Indigo has served on the board of directors or advisers for several non-profits, worked as staff or as a volunteer with numerous other organizations, and currently helps a wide range of non-profits and businesses take advantage of resources that can help them achieve their missions most effectively.

Indigo sees her writing as part of her service mission. In her writing she combines professional training with 25 years of spiritual study and practice and wisdom gained through helping herself and others face and transform challenging life experiences, to guide and support readers in their own journey of personal transformation and triumph.

www.ingramcontent.com/pod-product-compliance
Lightning Source LLC
Chambersburg PA
CBHW071658090426
42738CB00009B/1574